The Indomitable Simone Irene McMahon

Copyright © 2024 Jennifer McMahon

The moral right to be identified as the creators of the work has been asserted by them in accordance with the Copyright, Designs and Patents Act 1988. All rights reserved.

No part of this book may be reproduced, stored in a retrieval system or transmitted in any form or by any means, electronic, mechanical, photocopying, recording or otherwise, without the prior permission of Jennifer McMahon.

ISBN: 978-0-646-70260-5

Designed by Red Feather Publishing

www.redfeather.com.au

All proceeds of the book donated to charity.

For distribution enquiries please email: bookenquiries@hotmail.com

Contents

Chapter	
Introduction	2
1. The World Welcomes Simone Irene	4
2. The Making of a Legend...	10
3. Astute, Empowered, Effervescent and Tenacious	25
4. A Life of Service	37
5. Simone: Strong, Brave – Indomitable	46
6. Highlights of Simone's Life	51
7. Making Every Occasion Special	58
8. The Pandemic	71
9. A Race Against Time To Survive...	76
10. The Fight and Flight of a Butterfly	97
11. A Treasury of Tributes	99
12. Photos of Simone's Life	164

In loving memory of Simone

With many thanks to the various contributors to the book

Introduction

The story of a remarkable young woman, who defied immense odds to embark on a journey to stand up for her beliefs.

This story is a kaleidoscope of glorious memories each one more beautiful than the other. Like a garland of sweet-smelling blossoms, it depicts the essence of a life filled with a multitude of thunderstorms, but amidst the gloomy downpour there were also rainbows depicting the joy of living and embracing every minute of every day with boundless energy filled with fun and laughter whilst striving to avoid the clouds of sadness that rolled by intermittently due to her illness.

Like a palette of paint filled with different colours, this young lady endeavoured to paint each day with vibrant colours to transform the canvas of her life of chaos and pain into a masterpiece that depicted fun and laughter with every brush stroke, never letting go of the brush so she remained in control of every brush stroke of her life.

As you turn the pages, you will be driven to delve into this life that was so well lived, only to be amazed at the character of this remarkable young lady. She never let herself succumb to negativity, despair and setbacks but rose above her life of challenges and used each setback as a stepping stone to become a beacon of light to the vulnerable, providing a voice for them.

A heartwarming book that captivates and takes you on an emotional roller-coaster of laughter and tears. It will tug at your heart strings because of the strength and resilience of this family who overcame insurmountable obstacles to just survive.

The strength and closeness of this family's love for each other stood the test of time and you will definitely be inspired.

The World Welcomes Simone Irene

They say life is a series of thousands of tiny miracles and on the 9th of June 1982, one such miracle made her debut into the world… little Simone Irene. Her life became a journey of overcoming insurmountable obstacles, challenges and monumental triumphs that gave rise to incomprehensible achievements whilst laughing in the face of adversity. Simone went against the grain and that was what made her unique in so many ways, with the most alluring attribute of all… confidence. Simone had an abundance of it.

The day Simone came into Jennifer and Patrick's life, they were absolutely thrilled and excited, like all couples are at the birth of their first child. The couple say, Simone redefined their understanding of happiness. The moment they held Simone in their arms, they vowed to become Simone's shield of protection and acknowledge they were encapsulated with a feeling of pride and responsibility, crafted with a deep, unique bond that stood the test of time.

Unfortunately for them, their joy was shattered when they were told how sick their little baby was. Through the tears of joy came tears of despair, but they vowed between them that however bad it looked, they would rejoice in Simone's birth and battle on, regardless of the pessimistic views that surrounded them. The young couple vowed to devote their lives to seeing their bundle of joy through what was to be the battle of her life. It became their crusade; that Simone was not only going to "survive" as the doctors said, but she was going to win all life's battles. United, they fought every single one.

Then one day, while Simone was still in hospital, the parents were called in for a meeting. Patrick was at work and Jennifer says when she was called in to face four specialists, she had no idea what to expect. She remembers how an elderly nurse ran to the bassinet, wrapped up little baby Simone, and put her into Jennifer's arms and said, "now go in".

Jennifer recalls she walked in with her beautiful baby in her arms. It was the day the specialists had decided to inform the young mother that it was their opinion that her baby was not going to survive the week. Jennifer remembers looking down at her beautiful baby's face, and looking up at them and saying, "she believed that where there's life there's hope, and no one knows what tomorrow brings, none of us do, life is uncertain, but we should never give up hope". Jennifer remembers informing the specialists, she had no plans to give up on her baby's life, and it was her expectation that her yearning to save her baby's life would resonate with them.

Jennifer remembers walking out of the conference, confident her little Simone was going to survive, and as she looked at her cute face, she recalls that Simone looked up at her and "cooed", it felt like she said, "thank you, Mummy"!!

That day, Jennifer recalls she may have ruffled feathers by insisting they not give up on saving her baby's life, a plea any young mother would make. However, she was unaware that day was the start of ruffling a lot of feathers to fight for Simone all the way, with doctors, teachers, lecturers, classroom bullies and other people who tried to break that fabulous spirit that Simone had, that clearly told the world… "I will survive". Coincidentally, those words became a favourite karaoke song for Simone and her best friends!!

Patrick and Jennifer came to a decision then that Jennifer would have to give up her job if Simone was going to make it. The couple said Simone was their miracle and miracles happen once in a lifetime, so they were not going to give up on their "little miracle".

The young couple recall that they had just built their home and with it came the mortgage. They realised that they were going to suffer financially, as they had furnished their house completely, thinking Jennifer would return to work after maternity leave. It was a decision that was necessary, and they say they have no regrets whatsoever on their decision. The couple believe if anything, it is only during the hard times that true strength shines through, and this proved so true for they did not know how resilient they really were, till their resilience was really challenged.

They recall there were times while they were in hospital, when they had to share a meal, as they did not have enough money. Even though life became intolerable sometimes, having each other helped them cope. They believe that's where they built that wonderful bond between the three of them, as they would take their little bundle of joy with them for meals and walks in the hospital grounds. They feel certain that wonderful bond grew strong, from the time they spent together in the hospital facing the issues that surrounded them every day.

The couple say they were aware that they were the only ones who had faith, that the day would come when they would take their beautiful little baby home, even though pessimism surrounded them. They passionately believe their strong united bond was what helped them overcome the insurmountable challenges that plagued them throughout their stay in hospital, whilst they struggled to bring their baby home. They said they never gave up hope, confident that they would bring their baby home, even though the times were tough and challenging. The difficulties they faced made them more steadfast and determined to achieve their main objective which was taking little Simone home!

They prayed fervently for the day to take her home. Every smile little Simone gave, they say, helped them cope and their despair disappeared. The couple say Simone was a real "smiler."

Her smile melted their hearts and those around her. Jennifer says she remembers whenever Simone smiled, they would be thrilled with their baby's "smile", they say the nurses thought they were crazy parents, but what the nurses did not realise was that for the couple every smile was a sign of "HOPE' in their troubled world of despair.

The wonderful nursing staff boosted their determination to defy adversity. They were all mothers and helped the young couple to cope. Jennifer and Patrick say, they are forever grateful to those nurses for helping them through those very challenging early days.

All their life, the couple say, they had a strong belief in the powerful force of "Hope". Jennifer and Patrick believe that if you hope tomorrow will be better, it helps you get through the difficult moments of today, and things do come together. It finally did and the day arrived when the excited young couple took their beautiful baby daughter home and were absolutely thrilled to have her home.

The Making of a Legend...

Growing, learning and never taking no for an answer...

Simone came home and blossomed into a state of boundless energy. You could not limit her, and you could not underestimate her. From a young age, Simone embraced obstacles, eliciting to accept things that she could not change, whilst portraying resilience as her greatest weapon. She just became the best version of herself, and brought a lot of joy and laughter, whilst making a unique and profound impact on all those she met.

As a baby, Simone became the light in the lives of not only her parents, but the whole family especially as she was the first baby in the family. As a toddler, she looked like a walkie-talkie doll. Most people nicknamed her "Dolly," as she looked like a little doll with her lovely curls and her little walk, coupled with an amazing ability to talk non-stop at a very early age.

Simone just loved her whole family, and enjoyed the affection from her adoring parents, grandparents, her three uncles and her aunts, who showered her with gifts. Simone had her father wrapped around her little finger, and he was utterly bewitched from the moment Simone was put into his arms on the day she was born.

As a child Simone brought sunshine and laughter to the whole family, as she enjoyed imitating "Bennie Hill". Simone also enjoyed entertaining the family with her "magic shows" and would make them all sit and watch her perform her magic tricks, not forgetting to take the hat around after her magic show performance!

At the age of four, Simone joined a modelling school. The family recalls seeing the little Simone modelling was sheer delight, as she would forget that she was not supposed to talk, but only walk the walk! However, the little talkative Simone would always enjoy waving or taking off her sunglasses to wave at the family in the audience. Even the teacher used to find it amusing that the little Simone just could not stop herself from acknowledging her family. She would tell her teacher, "I wanted my family to know that I could see them".

Simone's young uncle and aunt bought her a keyboard. The young Simone soon became adept at playing the keyboard with the assistance of Jennifer's mum, who says Simone was an absolute delight to teach. She had this great thirst for learning at a very early age, and her nanny and parents harnessed that, and encouraged her to tackle whatever caught her attention.

When the local shopping centre ran a "Talent Quest" competition, Jennifer and Patrick entered the young Simone in the competition. She played her rendition of "In the Mood" on her keyboard. Simone was never intimidated by the stage and absolutely delighted the audience.

Life had become a struggle for the young family, as Jennifer had given up her job as she had decided it was imperative to stay home and bring up the delightful little Simone. Having built a new home, the mortgage started to cripple them financially, and their only hope was to find a way to supplement the family income.

Jennifer realised that she had to find a career that enabled her to work from home, to help with the finances whilst making sure Simone's needs were met. The couple's love of their daughter was always amplified, when any decision was made, and their daughter had the same amazing love for her parents that stood the test of time, making all those who knew this delightful family remain in awe, of their unconditional love for each other.

People noticed that this close-knit family link was strong and unique as they were able to tackle many obstacles in the ensuing years because of their bond of love for each other. Their love and determination to embrace challenges together was evident in everything they did. It was as beautiful as a symphony.

Jennifer said she eventually settled on doing a cake decorating course, as the owner of the cake shop allowed her to take the little Simone along with her to the classes. With great determination, Jennifer became a professional cake decorator, enabling her to work from home to help supplement their income. She recalls, how she used to pack up a mat, colour pencils and books for the little Simone, however it was of no interest to Simone as she was determined to be given a roll of icing, so she could follow the cake decorating teacher instead, much to the amusement of the teacher and other members of the class.

Simone was a fast learner and watched her mother decorating her beautiful creations, making all the floral decorations herself, and it was not long before Simone was helping to make the flowers for the cakes. At one stage, Jennifer and Patrick say they found they were constantly running out of toilet paper, and only found out why, when on Mother's Day the young Simone gave her mum a bunch of toilet paper roses, beautifully crafted by her. Jennifer says that was the most meaningful bouquet of roses she has ever received, as it was made with such a lot of love.

When little Simone turned six, she started school at Notre Dame Primary School. Simone was an intelligent student. It was at Notre Dame Primary School that Simone won her first award, "The Little Aussie of the Year" award, and Simone came home all smiles with her certificate. After that initial competition, Simone was again chosen to represent the school in the "Penguin Speak Up-Awards", with a speech that highlighted the current issues at that time.

Simone chose recycling as her topic, as at that time it was quite a lot in the news. However, Simone's recycling speech had a twist, as it was not about recycling the bottles and the cans to save the environment, it was about recycling organs to save the human race.

It was a heartfelt speech, spoken with an amazing sense of feeling and enthusiasm. It was also the first brush stroke on a canvas of a life, that was to become a map that was hard to navigate and visualise for someone who had defied all medical odds. Below is the speech:

RECYCLING

We hear a lot about recycling these days, saving the cans, the bottles, saving the environment and the endangered species, but sadly not much thought is given to saving the human race itself, by making people more aware of the significance of Organ Donation.

Please don't get me wrong, I am not against recycling, saving the environment or the endangered species. We definitely need to do our utmost to save our planet for future generations, but sadly we tend to forget that something can also be done to ease human suffering by the kind donation of the "Gift of Life".

Knowing that you have the power to change the quality of life for someone whose life depends on a machine to breathe, or a child whose existence depends on being hooked up to a machine to survive or having to take up to 15 to 20 tablets a day just to be able to go to work or school, things that healthy people take for granted. Who wouldn't want to use that power to do something. Wouldn't you?

It is just that people are not being made aware of the significance of Organ Donation. Maybe if they heard the statistics, they would realise how drastic the situation really is. In 1993, 367 people received organ transplants compared to a waiting list of 1,579 ending June 1993.

Australia unfortunately has the lowest organ donation rate in the developed countries, as a mere 12% per one million of population.

Maybe, just maybe, if all these facts were known, it would make people aware that it would be a wonderful way to depart from this world, by leaving their organs behind and I am sure God won't mind if you leave your organs behind.

I have been told that signing those donor cards and drivers' licences are just not enough. You have got to discuss your decision with your next of kin, because they are the ones who make that final decision.

In conclusion, I can only hope that I have got at least one of you considering the prospect, and if I haven't, then maybe these words from Robert Test will inspire you.

Give my sight to the man who has never seen a sunrise.

Give my heart to a person whose own heart has caused nothing but pain.

Give my kidneys to the one who depends on a machine to exist.

Give my sins to the devil and my soul to God.

If you must bury something, let it be my faults, my weaknesses, and all my prejudices against my fellow men

If by chance you wish to remember me, do it with a kind deed or word to someone who needs you

If you do, I shall live forever

Now, if you are still not inspired, I should add that I am forever thankful to the person who cared enough to change my life by giving me the "Gift of Life".

Simone McMahon

Notre Dame Primary School, 1994.

While still at Notre Dame Primary School, Simone's poorly functioning kidney gave up. Luckily for Simone, the doctor's prediction that her kidney would give up when she was 2 years old did not happen and her kidney only failed when she was 9 years old. Sadly, Simone had to go on dialysis, and the challenges that her parents faced when she was born, had now catapulted on to the vibrant young Simone, and she had to do dialysis whilst trying to create some type of normalcy to accommodate the regime of schooling.

School became a challenge for Simone and her parents trying to integrate dialysis, homework and doctor's appointments, whilst also having to deal with the schoolyard bullies. Jennifer believes her admiration for her daughter grew with the courage she showed to face those schoolyard bullies. Even though Simone was so tired after a whole night of dialysis, she still made it to school in the morning, whilst striving to achieve academically. Jennifer and Patrick say they remain forever proud of their beautiful daughter as Simone's challenges were many, but her triumphs were soon proven to be monumental.

Simone continued dialysis during the night so she could keep up with her schoolwork. Jennifer and Patrick say life became a real challenge for the young Simone doing dialysis during the night and getting to school in the morning. Being a kidney patient made her small in stature and prey to the awful school-yard bullies, who showed the young Simone no compassion for the hard life of being on dialysis all night, whilst still having to attend full-time school in the morning.

Jennifer says her heart ached for the pain and anxiety those school-yard bullies caused Simone but remembers that Simone never wanted mum Jennifer to intervene. Jennifer believes that's what probably motivated Simone to grow up and become a strong advocate for injustice to vulnerable people!

It was in Year 6 at the age of 11 while still at Notre Dame Primary School, Simone received a cadaver kidney transplant. Jennifer and Patrick are forever thankful to the caring staff and Community of Notre Dame Primary School, the then Principal Sr. Catherine Ryan, Simone's amazing and caring teachers Mrs Nannette Pethick, Mr Steve Doohan, Mr Glen Wilkinson and her ever caring Year 2 teacher the late Mrs Jenny Paul who even offered to give Simone one of her kidneys, but sadly she was not compatible.

Simone had her transplant, and even though she was transplanted with a poorly matched kidney, Simone's life was transported from just existing to living again. Simone crafted a life for herself that was proven to be unique, whilst making a profound impact on the lives of many.

After primary school, Simone joined St. Norbert College where she joined the Drama Class, and her love of theatre grew with her Drama teacher, Kerri Hilton. Simone enjoyed being in the theatre productions at St. Norbert College and became a keen thespian. Simone soon became a part of many theatre productions in local theatre companies around Perth, even getting her father Patrick to join her in the theatre performances.

Whilst in High School, Simone also thoroughly enjoyed her debating classes as well, even entering many debating competitions. They say a good speech is like a pencil, it must have a point, and most would strongly agree that Simone just had an amazing ability to get her point across.

Simone just loved the art of public speaking. It was a passion of hers which motivated her to try to excel in the skill, and eventually become a professional public motivational speaker. Simone was very comfortable in front of an audience. Besides becoming a professional motivational speaker, Simone also started giving public speaking lessons. Simone never wasted a minute of her day; it was always filled with some endeavour.

It was at St. Norbert College that Simone met two of her best friends, Emma and Rebecca. It was Simone who motivated the two girls to join her in entering the school's talent competitions, and even encouraged Emma to co-host the Talent Quest. With Rebecca, she encouraged her to take part in a boot-scooting competition, much to the surprise of Rebecca herself. Simone's two friends said that it was very hard to say 'no' to Simone as she was always very convincing!!

While at St. Norbert's College, Simone went from strength to strength with her newfound vigour after her kidney transplant. She became involved in all the school's activities. It was at St. Norbert College that Simone won her second and third awards, the Principals Medallion and the schools Citizenship Award. Simone finished High School in 1999 and left for university.

Simone went to the Notre Dame University to do her Bachelor of Laws degree. It was here that Simone met her third friend, Viede as well as Andrew Baker. Simone enjoyed her university days with Viede's friendship. Whenever they had free lecture classes, they would ride the free bus around Fremantle, and enjoy the sights, not forgetting the trips to the 'Golden Arches' the great McDonalds restaurant situated right on the beach in those days.

Simone also had a good friend in Andrew Baker, and she was thrilled that she and Andrew shared a strong love of the theatre, especially musicals. Simone was absolutely ecstatic when Andrew got her involved in the musical production of "Grease" at the Regal Theatre. Her parents said Simone always came home tired, but absolutely jubilant to be working as Assistant Stage Manager, for the production of "Grease".

Simone enjoyed her university days even though going to Notre Dame University meant she had to catch the Circle Route bus, which took an hour to get there. Going to university in those days was hard for Simone to carry all those heavy law books around when she got off the bus and had another long walk to the university. However, Simone was always cheerful and never ever complained. Simone was very pleased to have met and made two very good friends in Viede and Andrew, whilst she was studying Law at Notre Dame University.

After Simone left university, she worked at several legal jobs before finally settling into the area of Family Law.

Another of Simone's great loves was to travel and as soon as she received her transplant aged 11 years old, Simone could not wait to travel. Her first trip overseas was when her parents fulfilled their promise and took her to Disneyland, Hawaii and Las Vegas. Simone loved the experience and after that trip, she well and truly caught the 'travel bug'.

Simone couldn't wait to turn 14, that golden age when she was able to work, and predictably she got herself a job. So, every Thursday night for late night shopping, and on Saturdays, Simone would work diligently, at times holding down three different jobs, Big W, Harvey Norman, and Mazzuchelli's the Jewellers. The jewellers required her to acquire skills of the various types of jewellery, and she had to pass a small course that taught her about the different types of stones and how they were cut to make up various jewellery items. At Big W, she became a 'checkout chick', eventually getting her friend Emma to join her.

At Harvey Norman, she was a salesperson doing her best to sell as much as she could, to earn a small commission on her sales. Her Harvey Norman boss recalls how he spotted her one day working at Big W and remembers asking her why she was working at Big W also, and he remembers Simone saying, "maybe if you gave me more hours, I would not need to work at Big W as well."

Simone was fiercely independent and responsible and made use of every day accomplishing something. She gave tuitions in English and Maths and gave Piano lessons and Public Speaking lessons as well. She was also a professional Public Speaker and was booked regularly, which was another source of income for her travel. Wherever she could, Simone endeavoured to capitalise on all her skills to earn extra money to save for her little travel ventures.

Jennifer and Patrick sadly recall that her biggest travel dream was to visit Santorini one day, but unfortunately it wasn't meant to be. Patrick and Jennifer say they used to watch in amusement whenever Simone came home from work, she would be like the legendary King in his counting house counting all the money, keeping a close check on her little bank account!

Simone was an excellent saver, but never ever stingy, always very happy to give, to make others happy… an admirable trait. She just loved the joy of giving. When she started working at 14 years old, her first pay went to buy Christmas presents for all her little cousins and her parents and grandparents. Simone also gave a lot of her time freely for charity, like public speaking events for Rotary Clubs and other charitable organisations. She was always willing to assist whenever called upon. Every time she travelled, she made sure she brought back presents for everyone she loved.

Simone had this amazing drive to make use of every hour of every day accomplishing something, and her parents found it hard to keep up with their little human dynamo.

They recall how one day, Simone decided to join the W.A. Young Labour group. The organisation was to interest young people in political and social action. Jennifer and Patrick said it was one time they had to suggest to Simone to please call a halt to this new venture, as the meetings were too far from where they lived, and they felt it was not safe for her to drive the distance. Simone very reluctantly agreed and dropped out.

Astute, Empowered, Effervescent and Tenacious

...words that describe Simone best

Simone was a very pretty young woman, with beautiful almond shaped brown eyes, glistening dark hair and exotic features. Despite her steely core, she was a 'girly girl' at heart, who loved to shop for clothes and jewellery. She chose bright colours to reflect her personality and was always exceptionally well-presented. Simone also loved to laze by the pool, or visit the beach, a rare respite from her busy schedule.

Even though Simone was very petite, not quite 5 feet tall; she was a veritable pocket rocket. What she lacked in stature, she made up for in love, courage, loyalty, mischief, playfulness, feistiness, and determination when called for. She never backed away from a challenge, whether she was fighting for herself, or standing up for others who did not have the needed resources or energy. She did whatever was required to accomplish a goal because of her tenacious personality.

Simone had an amazing effervescent personality, always full of fun and her friends remember her always being ready to tackle anything, that sometime even proved out of their comfort zone, but the dynamic Simone was hard to refuse.

Simone proved to be an excellent student, popular with her schoolmates for her sense of fun and exceptional mimicking talents, even taking off their Irish principal in primary school to a tee to her classmates' amusement. Humbled and inspired by Simone's courage and zest for life, her three closest friends reluctantly attempted and excelled at the missions Simone encouraged them to do. Simone was incredibly driven to succeed despite the setbacks in life.

As soon as Simone turned 21, her parents took her to celebrate her 21st birthday in Melbourne. Her birthday gift included a stay for one night at the Crown Towers. Simone asked if she could invite her friend Becky to join them on the trip, as they wanted to go to Mt. Buller to see snow.

Jennifer and Patrick still remember the dejected faces of the two girls, when they arrived at the Crown Towers in Melbourne because the flight from Perth to Melbourne was delayed, so when they went to check in to their room, they were told that their room had been given to another guest because of their late arrival. The hotel had assumed that they were no longer going to arrive. The girls looked at each other disappointedly. However, the man at the desk, realising the error, asked the girls if they would like an upgrade to their room. Jennifer and

Patrick recall how amusing it was to see the speed at which the girls agreed to the upgrade. To their utter delight and amazement, when they opened the door to the upgraded hotel room, they were thrilled to see that they had been upgraded to the "Penthouse suite".

The girls ran excitedly from room to room, squealing in delight as they had never been in a suite before! The tap on the door put the icing on the cake when this massive basket of goodies arrived with champagne and chocolates. Simone was absolutely thrilled to receive the goodies being her 21st birthday. Jennifer remembers them saying how happy they were that the flight had been delayed! The girls reckon that the day was a momentous day never to be forgotten!

The 21st birthday gift was for only a one-night stay at the Crown Towers since they had planned to spend 10 days in Melbourne. They had booked an apartment for the rest of the trip. The girls had quickly grown accustomed to the luxury of the Penthouse, and Jennifer and Patrick said it was sad to see the girls' faces when they had to lower their standards and move from the Crown Towers to the little apartment for the rest of the trip!

However, the excitement of being on their first trip in Melbourne made them get over the disappointment of leaving the luxury of the Crown Towers, and it wasn't long before they settled into the little apartment. Jennifer and Patrick remember coming back from shopping to find the two girls dancing with the brooms in their hands to John Farnham's 'Sadie, the cleaning lady' on the night of John Farnham's Melbourne concert. Although they couldn't attend the concert, the girls were happy that the apartment was situated so close to the venue that they could clearly hear John Farnham singing, so they made the most of it.

After returning from Melbourne, Simone got herself a full-time job. Her parents recall their daughter came home from work one day, and gave them an envelope and said excitedly, "open it up quickly." Jennifer and Patrick said they were left speechless when they opened it up, as they realised how hard Simone must have saved, as the envelope contained three round-the-world tickets. Her parents were overwhelmed with emotion, realising how hard their precious daughter had worked to save up the amount needed for the family tickets. They were soon to discover that Simone had booked all the holiday destinations including back-to-back tours. The extensive itinerary was exhausting. Simone had never booked a holiday before, so Jennifer and Patrick were amazed at how well she had managed to book all accommodation and tours by herself. She became so proficient at making travel arrangements that before long the family was travelling at short notice due to the deals Simone somehow managed to secure for them! Patrick ran into a lady who works at the local travel agency who was not aware that Simone had passed away. The lady was devastated to hear the sad news but told Patrick that she had been so impressed by Simone's ability to find the best deals and plans and book holidays that she had offered Simone a job. She could see that Simone had a talent for sourcing great deals and putting together holiday packages, so she thought that Simone would be a great asset to the business. Travel agent was just another one of Simone's hidden talents.

Simone loved the United States, and her favourite city was New York, and she visited three times. She had a strong love for the iconic "Times Square" and was totally captivated as her love of Broadway came to the fore. Broadway highlighted Simone's love of musical theatre, and she spent most of her time going from theatre to theatre. Broadway provided a smorgasbord of musicals, and Simone was utterly captivated with the theatre district. Jennifer and Patrick say Simone was out every night taking in a show. The iconic theatre district of Broadway became one of the highlights of Simone's travels.

Simone also enjoyed her trip to Memphis, Tennessee, to visit Elvis Presley's mansion. She was absolutely thrilled to also stroll down the popular "Beale Street" in the heart of downtown Memphis that showcases the melting pot of the delta blues, jazz, rock "n" roll, R&B and not forgetting the gospel. Simone had to stop and check out all the restaurants, eventually deciding on "Hard Rock Cafe" as it looked lots of fun. "Beale Street" was well worth the visit, according to Simone, as she thoroughly enjoyed the jazz players and all the sights and music during her stay in Memphis.

Even though Simone had put Memphis on her itinerary just for her dad, who is an avid Elvis fan, Patrick said he was so pleased to see how much Simone enjoyed her time on the Elvis Presley tour. Simone had booked the family into the "Heartbreak Hotel" and the fun-loving Simone thoroughly enjoyed herself with the activities at the hotel, and the tour of Elvis Presley's Graceland mansion, admitting to her dad that she had become an Elvis fan after her exposure to the wonderful Elvis Presley Tour.

Patrick fondly remembers how his delightful daughter had secretly booked him in to record his voice on a CD at the legendary 'Sun Studio' as a special treat, saying "dad now you can tell everyone, you did a recording of your voice in the same studio that Elvis recorded his voice!" Simone was so thrilled to see how much Patrick enjoyed the experience.

Knowing she had to do something for mum as well, Simone secretly booked a wedding chapel in Las Vegas for her parents to renew their wedding vows. Without telling Jennifer, she organised for an "Elvis" impersonator to walk her down the aisle while he sang "Can't help falling in love with you" much to the embarrassment of Jennifer, who Simone knew would never have agreed to it, as she knew mum hated the limelight, so she kept it top secret!

Even dad, was not in on the secret, as she was afraid of him letting out her surprise. Simone told her parents she was taking them to a special place, and they needed to be in formal wear. Her parents say they were shocked when the Elvis impersonator met them at the entrance to the chapel, and gave Jennifer a bouquet and whisked her away, while Simone accompanied her dad Patrick into the chapel. Jennifer and Patrick looked over at Simone, and she was chuckling away to see her mum's face when the Elvis impersonator was walking and singing her down the aisle, while she was happily recording everything with great amusement.

Jennifer and Patrick also recall when they went to Paris how their lovely daughter organised a trip down the "Seine" telling her dad to make sure when the song of "Under the Bridges of Paris" started he must give her mum a kiss, or as she always jokingly called it, a "wedding kiss." Simone always thought of every little detail when organising a travel adventure, making sure that all three of them enjoyed the trip. Patrick and Jennifer were always surprised at Simone's little "packages of fun" for each trip.

There was always some surprise when Simone organised anything. Even her friends would agree that Simone would always make sure that everything had to have that element of "fun."

Simone also enjoyed her trips to the UK, where she fulfilled her dream of being in the world-renowned Shakespeare's Globe Theatre located on the banks of the river Thames in London. There was only one ticket left on that day, and Simone's parents knew that Simone had waited years to be inside Shakespeare's Globe Theatre, so they gave her the chance to fulfil her dream while they waited outside for her at a local café on the banks of the river Thames. They were not surprised to see Simone come out ecstatic and smiling with delight, talking non-stop, describing the thrill of being inside Shakespeare's Globe Theatre.

Simone also made sure she took in all the musicals offered in London, especially the ones that she had missed in New York, so every night it was "show time" for Simone and her parents. Simone's passion for musicals was truly fulfilled by her visits to New York and London.

Simone loved the thrill of bringing joy to others, and so when she visited Venice, she remembered how her grandmother's greatest wish was to visit Venice. As soon as Simone got to Venice and sat in the Gondola, she told the gondolier how much her grandmother wanted to see Venice, and somehow managed to convince the gondolier to sing "Santa Lucia" while he manoeuvred the gondola down the canal, and Simone rang her grandmother and said, "Nanny as you cannot come to Venice, I am bringing Venice to you" and she held her mobile phone so the gondolier could sing for her nanny. It was 2 o'clock in the morning in Perth but her grandmother was absolutely thrilled, calling it a veritable feast for her ears, and says she was so overwhelmed with the love and caring Simone had shown in this wonderful caring gesture.

Recalling Simone's love of bringing joy to others, Simone surprised her parents with a trip to Broome. Jennifer and Patrick recall how Simone came home one day and announced she had booked a short trip away to Broome. It was her parents' 40th wedding anniversary. When they got to Broome, the parents were surprised when their loving daughter took them to the beach. Waiting for them on the beach was a wedding celebrant standing under a beautiful wedding canopy facing the stunning ocean, against the backdrop of a glorious sunset. Simone took out a beautiful bouquet of ruby roses to depict the 40th wedding anniversary colour she had made herself, and a beautiful wreath of flowers for her mum's hair, which she handed to her mum and a buttonhole for her dad. The parents say that they remember how Simone had her room door locked for days. It was only when they got to Broome they realised the reason for the locked room door, as she was busy making the floral gifts for her mum and dad.

After the ceremony, Jennifer and Patrick say their loving daughter booked dinner for the three of them in a restaurant on the beach. The parents say, though there were only the three of them, they were so very happy to share that special day in their life together with the most precious person in their life, their beautiful daughter. Simone had this wonderful trait of always surprising her parents with special gestures of love. It is no wonder that this family caught the attention of many people, as they were truly a unique story that depicted a love and togetherness, that pulled at the heartstrings when you met them.

Besides her great love of travelling, Simone also loved her music, having a special place in her heart for John Farnham. From the young age of four, Simone became an ardent fan of John Farnham, and developed a strong love of his music, knowing the words to all his songs. It is fair to say that the great loves of Simone's life were John Farnham and her wonderful parents, not in that order.

Another great love of Simone's was her basketball team, "The Wildcats". From about the age of six, she became a very enthusiastic fan of the "Wild Cats" This was the period of some of her heroes, such as James Crawford, Cal Bruton and Mike

Ellis, to name a few. Her young uncle bought her a "Wild Cats" jacket when she was only seven years old. Jennifer and Patrick recall how thrilled Simone was when she got her jacket and looked after it really well.

Simone and her dad Patrick became basketball "buddies" and were soon dressed in full gear, attending all the "Wildcats" games. They never missed a single home game of the "Wildcats". Patrick and Simone enjoyed going to the basketball games together, however Simone was a little miffed when people asked her if she was Patrick's wife!! A compliment for Patrick, but Simone wasn't so sure!

Another event that Simone loved was the 'Crab Festival' held in Mandurah, W.A. each year. Simone couldn't wait to book the family into this annual event. For Simone, it wasn't the appeal of the crabs, because she did not eat crabs, but it was to soak up the atmosphere of the different cultures offering an array of foods and talent in a fun atmosphere. It always gave the fun-loving Simone, a real buzz to stroll through the festival. There weren't many things that Simone disliked.

Her condition and awareness of others gave her a special empathy to understand aspects of human nature. The one and only area that Simone could not accept was being treated unfairly.

Jennifer and Patrick hope they can carry on Simone's legacy of fighting for justice by opening a centre in Simone's honour, so vulnerable people have access to help them in troubled times. Jennifer and Patrick say they have never bought so many lotto tickets, hoping their vision can one day become a reality.

In 2007, Simone was selected for a Churchill Fellowship and travelled to the United States, the United Kingdom and concluded in Spain. Following her Churchill Fellowship, Simone returned home with renewed vigour and in the next few years, Simone thrived academically, socially, and most importantly physically.

Simone was so very grateful for her lifesaving organ transplant, and she became aware of the many who were awaiting transplant operations, that she decided to dedicate her life to increasing community awareness of the need for organ and tissue donation, so others could enjoy life without the restraints of dialysis and being hooked up to a machine to survive.

A Life of Service

Simone seems to have had a formula that her life had a purpose, and the essence of her life was to be of service with the ability to influence change with a determination for the common good.

Following her transplant, Simone continued her voluntary work with renewed vitality, strength, and enthusiasm for several organisations, most notably Transplant Australia and the Starlight Children's Foundation and then for her very own Foundation which she founded herself, The Organ Donation and Transplant Foundation of W.A. Simone was committed to improving the lives of people awaiting transplants, recipients, the families of posthumous donors, and living donors.

Simone was very passionate about promoting organ and tissue donation, so with the help of her very faithful group of volunteers, ran various charity events to highlight the profile of Organ and Tissue Donation. The various events included Quiz Nights, Debating Events, Art Exhibitions, Entertainment Book selling, Melbourne Cup Lunches,

Photography Exhibitions and, of course, the beautiful "Star Night."

It was Simone who started and organised the "Star Night" with the help of her faithful volunteers from her Foundation, The Organ Donation and Transplant Foundation of W.A. It was a special night, with the main objective being to provide a supportive platform for the recognition and acknowledgement of W.A. organ and tissue donors. "Star Night" was for the donor family community to get together, and have the opportunity to reflect, recognise and celebrate the "Gift of Life", only made possible by their kindness in agreeing to donate their family's organs and tissues.

The "Star Night" also enabled the donor families the chance to dedicate a "Star" on the night to honour their loved ones with the compassionate support of the Perth Observatory. It was a unique event for it brought the West Australian organ and tissue donor community together, to celebrate the spirit of giving, whilst honouring all W.A. organ and tissue donors who had given the ultimate gift... "The Gift of Life."

"The Star Night" was held at the Old Perth Observatory under the night sky, and sprinkled with the glow of the stars, it provided the ultimate solemnity for the beautiful candle lit dedication ceremony.

Simone also ran various charity events to raise the profile of organ donation, to try to boost organ donation rates in Western Australia. One such event was the "Great Debate" which was held in Forrest Chase at the old post office hall. It was a debating competition between various groups. One of the debating events which caught much attention was the event when the politicians and the medical fraternity took on the debating challenge. It was well received, with the aim to get people talking about organ donation, which was accomplished. The politicians won and walked away with the trophy.

Simone and her tireless volunteer workers from The Organ Donation and Transplant Foundation of W.A. worked extremely hard at fundraising, to enable them to succeed in all their endeavours, to raise awareness on organ and tissue donation as well as highlighting community awareness, of the number of people awaiting transplants.

The major fund-raising event was the "Sausage Sizzle" mornings run at various local locations with the help of all the hard-working volunteers of the Organ Donation and Transplant Foundation of W.A. Most say Simone's dedication to the cause was really inspiring and always had a profound impact on them.

Simone, together with the help of her trusted volunteers, were always ready and waiting for the next project such as the

"New Life" art and photography exhibition during Donate Life Week. It was at a busy local shopping centre that stories of hope and transformation were showcased, highlighting the importance of organ donation. Simone's mentorship and wisdom resonated with her young volunteers in shaping their own careers whilst they were volunteering at the Organ Donation and Transplant Foundation of W.A.

Various universities and schools also called upon Simone to speak to their students during their youth volunteering programs, as she was such a strong motivational speaker. Having her speak about her advocacy work portrayed her tireless efforts and resourcefulness in the field, providing that positive impact needed to encourage the young students to forge ahead with confidence whilst also encouraging them to become strong advocates and volunteers in their chosen fields.

As a wish-granting volunteer for the Starlight Children's Foundation, Simone was able to turn the dreams of seriously ill children into reality. She would work tirelessly to get companies to donate items that included cubby houses, aviaries, wheelchairs, bikes, and trips to Dream World on the Gold Coast in Queensland.

One little girl's greatest wish was to see snow, and as the little girl was unable to travel, Simone convinced a local ice-skating rink manager to make the rink look like it was snowing so the little girl could have her wish granted. The little girl was absolutely thrilled, and so was Simone, that through her efforts, a little girl's wish to see snow was granted.

On another occasion, there was a young boy who was very keen to play basketball at a professional level and needed a sports wheelchair to make it in the team. Simone worked hard to make sure he was able to get his wheelchair. Several years later Simone met him while shopping and was thrilled to hear that he had made it to professional basketball! These were only a few examples of the many wishes that were granted through Simone's unwavering dedication to grant all the wishes she was asked to do.

Simone was also involved in bringing the Transplant Games to Perth and worked very hard to help make it a success. She worked with her usual enthusiasm to help organise the event so that everyone could have a great time, and most would agree it was quite a mammoth feat that was well accomplished.

At the age of 21, Simone achieved a Bachelor of Laws Degree from the University of Notre Dame in Western Australia. Simone worked at many jobs finally settling as a Family Lawyer and worked in Family Law and Women's Advocacy. She had a passion for the welfare of children.

Simone excelled in her professional life but was always under the spectre of the challenges of living with renal failure, having occasional bouts of hospitalisation, and maintaining the rigorous regime of dialysis three times a week, but Simone seemed to thrive against every aspect of adversity. She was always positive and cheerful.

They say every adversity, every failure, every heartache carries with it the seed of an equal or greater outcome. For Simone that was so true as the numerous awards are testimony to that fact. Some of those amazing awards are mentioned below:

AWARDS AND MERITORIOUS RECOGNITION

<u>Member of the Order of Australia – AM</u> – for long-term contribution to the field of Organ and Tissue Donation.

<u>Winston Churchill Fellowship</u> – which enabled Simone to travel to the US, UK, and Spain to study the International Models of Organ and Tissue Donation.

<u>W.A. Young Australian of the Year in 2006 and 2008</u> – a national award recognising outstanding achievement in providing voluntary services to the community in the field of organ and tissue donation.

<u>Prime Ministers Centenary Medal</u> – This is an Australian commemorative medal, which marks the achievements of a

broad section of the Australian community for contribution to the Organ Donation and Transplant sector and for making our country and the wider world a better place.

Browne's W.A. Woman of the Year – in recognition of outstanding achievement as a Western Australian Woman.

Principal's Medallion – St. Norbert College – An award presented at graduation by the principal of the college to selected students to acknowledge outstanding achievements academically as well as in all other areas of community and college.

Citizenship Award – St. Norbert College – recognising outstanding contribution to the college, the church, and the wider community.

Lions Club Exemplary Service Award – Nominated by Victoria Park Lions Club for contribution to the W.A. community to the field of Organ and Tissue Donation.

Who's Who of Australia Member – A book of prominent individuals in Australia in celebration of all their achievements.

Scoop Magazine Inspirational West Australian of the Year

Australia's Representative for The American Young Leadership Dialogue in Washington DC

Community Newspaper Group – Recognises outstanding community service work in the field of Organ and Tissue Donation.

Penguin Speak Up Award – A public speaking competition for Primary Schools within W.A.

Best Production for the play Award – Independent Theatre Production – Youth Fest. Simone was a keen thespian and decided to try her hand as a Producer and was thrilled when she won the award.

Besides the numerous awards, Simone was also very involved in many Committees and Boards. Below are a few of them:

COMMUNITY SERVICE AND COMMITTEE/BOARD REPRESENTATION

Starlight Children's Foundation - Wish granting volunteer and National Executive advisory panel member

Transplant Australia – Vice Chair of the Australian Transplant Games Board

Transplant Australia – W.A. State President and National Director

Transplant Promotion Group W.A. – W.A. State President

Professional and motivational speaker/lecturer

In addition to her numerous awards and achievements, Simone was also extremely involved in various voluntary Boards and Advisory Groups in which she worked tirelessly.

These include:

W.A. Department of Health Renal Executive Advisory Group

Donate Life W.A. Organ and Tissue Donation Advisory Committee

International Society of Organ Donation Procurement Member

Consumer Representative of Renal Health Advisory Group

Member of the National Volunteer Advisory Panel Starlight Childrens Foundation

State President and National Director of Transplant Australia

Vice Chair and Local Organiser of the Perth Transplant Games

Patient Advocate

Member of the Youth Steering Committee

Simone: Strong, Brave – Indomitable

Simone is best described as indomitable, an epitome of strength and courage. Strong, brave and difficult to defeat or frighten. A true warrior, who fought relentlessly for justice for all vulnerable people. Simone truly believed transparency increased credibility and accountability and fought to the very end for those awaiting transplants despite her very own needs, due to the challenges of being on dialysis for 13 long years.

Simone was always up to any challenge and had a zest for life that enabled her to try her hand at everything. She had a deep love of life with a desire to enjoy the wonder and magic on what the world has to offer. Like a true butterfly whose wings of transformation are born out of struggle, Simone was proof that you can go through darkness yet become something beautiful.

Nothing daunted the fun-loving Simone. One day she heard an advertisement asking for people who would like to learn how to be a disc jockey on the radio, and as everyone who knew Simone would agree, it was very hard to say "no" to her if she had her mind made up to do something. So, after persuading her parents, she signed up for two whole weeks to train as a disc-jockey. Her parents say she came home jubilant after her night at the local radio station. With her usual gusto, Simone delved into the life of disc-jockeys and had herself a great time. As usual, her dad had a name for her. Every night she came through the door; he would say, here comes the "Happy Disc-jockey!"

Not long after her two weeks being a disc-jockey, she then decided she was very keen on taking a balloon modelling artistry course. She convinced her dad to go with her to learn to make balloons into various shapes. This time the excuse for taking the course was that it would help her in her role assisting the Starlight Children's Foundation. The course she took taught her how to make animal-shaped balloons, which she used to brighten children's days. Needless to say, her dad gave in to her request to accompany her. Simone shared her balloon-making skills with her neighbour's children as well, bringing much joy to those little ones who enjoyed the lovely balloon shapes she created.

Women like Simone have the grit, passion and persistence to go the distance to accomplish as much as possible. On another occasion, Simone's mum remembers, when her workplace was looking for a "Fairy" for the staff Christmas Party to entertain the staff kids, they asked if Simone would oblige. Simone was thrilled to do so, as her friends would attest; Simone just loved to dress up. She was asked if she wouldn't mind doing a bit of "Face Painting" as well if they provided the paints. Of course, Simone readily agreed, as nothing daunted Simone.

When she came home, she told her parents how much she enjoyed the experience of "Face Painting" which led her to doing a "Face Painting" course. It was not long after, she managed to convince her friend Emma to join her and dress up as a clown for various charity events.

On another occasion, Simone burst through the door at home with great enthusiasm and announced that she was seriously considering becoming a professional photographer. This time she convinced her dad to become her "caddy" to carry all the heavy photographic gear! "I will pay you a commission dad, if you are a good caddy she said!" Patrick says as usual he couldn't refuse her, especially when she looked up at him with those beautiful brown eyes. It was not long before she was doing weddings, pregnancy, engagements, and baby photos.

Ever the entrepreneur, Simone then saw an advertisement for a small wedding family business that was for sale. However, this time it was mum Jennifer's turn to be persuaded. Realising mum was not as easy as her dad to convince, Simone came prepared with a well-written pros and cons statement, outlining a 50/50 partnership arrangement between her and her parents. In the pitch to her mum, Simone explained to her mum that her artistic talent could be utilised, to turn the small business into a profitable income earner to help with the household finances.

As it was only a very small family business, the initial outlay was modest. Simone convinced mum Jennifer to contribute half of the sale price, and she would put in the other half, and they could buy it. Jennifer agreed, not realising at that time that Simone had great plans to build it up into a profitable income source to help the family finances.

Before long, she was building up the business, and their industrious 'little pocket rocket' daughter was off on another challenge; to bring in some wedding orders to reassure Jennifer that her investment had paid off. Simone always chose to see opportunities, not obstacles, and was always prepared with answers to any negative questions. It was not long before Jennifer was convinced that the investment was helping to support the household budget. Simone kept reminding her mum that she should use the artistic talents she was blessed with. "You should not waste the artistic talent you have inherited from Poppy", Simone gently chided.

Simone soon had the little family business up and running whilst slowly building it up, using only the profits from each wedding order. She basked in the compliments when they finished decorating each wedding venue. She would always ask Jennifer "Well Mum, aren't you pleased with the outcome" knowing how much her mother just loved using her artistic skills; but difficult financial and personal circumstances had prevented Jennifer from exploring her talents. Simone had an innate ability to always know how to bring out the best in others.

Highlights of Simone's Life

The highlights of Simone's life melded together to portray the happiest moments of a life well lived.

The crème-de-la crème of her achievements was when she was cited for the Member of the Order of Australia in Her Majesty the Queen's Honour List. To receive such a prestigious award at the very young age of 31 was indeed amazing. Her indefatigable efforts in promoting organ donation were at last extensively recognised and commended.

Simone was also absolutely thrilled and honoured to be announced the W.A. Young Australian of the Year in 2006, and then again in 2008. They were momentous nights to remember for Simone, her family and friends.

In 2006, together with seven other Young Australians of the Year, Simone's parents, relatives and friends, recall how proud they all were to see Simone carry in the Australian Flag, together with other Young Australians of the Year, in the presence of Her Majesty Queen Elizabeth II. They said it gave them a sense of utter pride to see Simone in the Commonwealth Games Flag Bearing Ceremony.

Simone was also thrilled and honoured when she received the Prime Minister's Centenary Medal and the following certificate:

To: Simone Irene McMahon

> "Whereas Her Majesty Queen Elizabeth The Second Queen of Australia has instituted an Australian Medal to commemorate the Centenary of Federation of Australia I Do by this warrant award you the Centenary Medal".

In 2018, Simone was one of the many West Australians chosen to carry the Queen's Baton through Perth in the final stages of its journey to the Gold Coast 2018 Commonwealth Games.

2006 and 2008 was another exciting time for the young Simone as she was able to take part in the Transplant Games in Geelong and Perth, receiving six medals in total, 1 Gold, 3 Silvers and 2 Bronze Medals for competing in table tennis and squash.

Becoming a Churchill Fellow was another highlight of Simone's life, as it enabled her to travel to the UK, US and Spain to study the models of Organ and Tissue Donation in the various countries and to identify and document successful models of organ and tissue donation. It enabled her to assess promotional strategies and programs that provide support to transplant recipients, donor families and living donors. Simone provided an exhaustive report, which outlined the various models from the countries visited. When she handed in her report, Simone's love of Churchill quotes was evident. On her report, she had one of Winston Churchill's quotes:

> "Success is not final; failure is not fatal: it is the courage to continue that counts."

Simone also got to travel to Washington DC, after being selected to be a part of the Young Australian Leadership Dialogue delegates, which enabled her to go to the White House.

Another highlight for Simone was being chosen to be featured in the "Who's Who" Book, which provides a unique perspective on extraordinary and prominent Australian individuals, detailing their accomplishments and leadership achievements.

In 1990, Simone was chosen to meet Sir Cliff Richard for an Art Studio visit in Claremont that was being hosted for him. Simone was thrilled to meet Sir Cliff Richard as she was familiar with his music as her mum Jennifer was an ardent fan of Sir Cliff since she was a youngster.

In 1993, it was the 25th Anniversary of Telethon, and a lot of international stars were invited to be part of the anniversary celebrations. Simone was chosen as one of the children of the hospital, to meet the iconic Celine Dion. It was a very young Celine Dion, and a very very young Simone!!

Simone had been a fan of John Farnham from a very young age and so when she got the opportunity to meet her favourite singer John Farnham, it was a very excited young Simone who just could not stop talking about the time she spent chatting with John Farnham when he came for a concert in Perth.

In 2006, Simone was invited to be Cinderella in the 2006 Channel Seven Christmas Pageant. She was absolutely delighted to be able to get to sit in the Cinderella's Carriage and get driven through the streets of Perth. Simone's mum and dad were thrilled to see their daughter so ecstatic and said she looked like a real princess in that carriage, and they were very proud parents.

Willingness was a trademark of Simone, so it was no surprise that when she was asked to speak on behalf of transplant recipients at the Tree Planting Ceremony, she readily agreed despite the fact, that she had never spoken publicly in front of such a large audience.

Her parents recall how the Chief Executive Officer of the Council asked for time to re-arrange the furniture to accommodate the next speaker, as he had to put a special stool so the little Simone could reach the microphone! Below is the speech by the young Simone on that day:

Not long ago my life was filled with numerous visits to the doctors, hospital, enough medicines to make me rattle, a real strict diet and, of course, being hooked up to the dialysis machine.... not a life I would wish for anyone!!!

Today, I enjoy life to the fullest, thankfully see less of doctors (no offence doctors), have no machine to tie me down, no more strict diets, which allows me to indulge myself with chocolates and I can safely say I don't rattle anymore, as there's not an abundance of tablets to take...and this wonderful change, is all thanks to one kind person, who cared enough to change the quality of my life.

It was the kind donation of the "Gift of Life" that enabled me to get a new kidney, which has made such a tremendous difference to my health.

So, I would like to pay a little tribute to that special person, who changed the quality of my life.

Special is a word that is used to describe something that's one of a kind...

Like a hug, or a sunset, or a person who spreads love, with a smile or a kind gesture.

Special describes people who act from the heart, and keep in mind the hearts of others.

Special applies to something that is admired and precious and which can never be replaced.

So, special is a word that describes YOU best.

The "Gift of Life" is such an enormous contribution that a person makes, for it's as many as nine people that benefit from the organ and tissue donation of just one person.

I think I speak for all recipients, when I say how thankful we are for this wonderful gift, and there's not a day that goes by when we are not aware of this.

I would now like to conclude with a remembrance....

We can't know why, the lily has so brief a time to bloom, before it folds its fragrance in, and bids the world goodnight

But we can know that nothing that is loved, is ever lost, for no one who has touched a heart, can really pass away...

Because some beauty lingers on, in each memory, that they have been a part of...

Making Every Occasion Special

Simone was like a bottle of champagne, effervescent and bubbly, so all celebratory occasions had that effervescent effect when she organised any occasion.

Simone just treasured all celebratory occasions. Coupled with Jen's creativity, she loved to dress the table in a festive theme. Simone especially loved High Teas, with delicate cakes and club sandwiches expertly displayed on occasions such as Mother's Day and Father's Day, complete with a beautifully presented menu! Birthdays and Easter were also given the Simone special touch. She never lost the magic of childhood, and the excitement and thrill of giving and receiving presents.

Simone's friends loved her birthday parties, as they knew that there would always be something unusual organised with this fun-loving friend of theirs. There was even a night of belly-dancing that the group of friends thoroughly enjoyed together with Simone, who came home and said she did not realise how much fun belly dancing really was.

There was also a Birthday party that Simone decided should be a "Masquerade Party". Everyone in the room was thrilled to be a part of that night with some very beautiful masks on show for the night. However, the highlight of that night was when one of the guests was nominated to announce that Simone was chosen to receive the Queen's Honour. It was a special treat for all those who loved Simone dearly and were thrilled for her to receive this well-deserved honour of the Member of the Order of Australia for all her hard volunteer work.

Simone's 30th birthday was another fun filled occasion. It was a night that transported everyone to a night in New York with the beautiful New York themed decorations. There were also the famous yellow cabs, as place card holders, which were painstakingly painted by Simone herself. It was an atmosphere of fun and laughter, with some people dressed as famous Hollywood stars and some in very unusual costumes.

To Simone's fun-loving delight, there was also a homeless person, often seen in "Times Square." Simone herself did not realise till one of the guests complained to Simone that there was a homeless person on the steps to the entrance of the venue. Simone went to check it out only to discover it was a guest and actually her very own aunt who did it to amuse the fun-loving Simone. Her aunt's children, Simone's young cousins, complained they were embarrassed to sit with their mum in the car on the way to the party and were hoping they did not get picked up for a traffic offence. Being the typical teenagers, they found it "embarrassing" to have their mum dress up like that.

Simone's whole family and her friends knew Simone's fun-loving nature. The family were all aware of how Simone loved fun, so another aunt dressed up as the Statue of Liberty. There even was a friend who dressed up as a sizzling "Hot Dog"!

To complement the night, Simone organised some beautiful New York special cocktails, much to the delight of her friends.

Simone's dad Patrick gave a special speech on that night, which was very heartwarming and loved by the guests. See below:

"A warm welcome to everyone on behalf of Simone's mum and me. Thank you so much for sharing in Simone's 30th birthday with us tonight. It just would not have been the same without all of you – for each one of you here tonight has in some way played an important role in Simone's life.

Thirty years has seen Simone through many milestones. We have seen baby years turning into toddling years. We have seen Simone learning to talk and walk – unsteady at first but growing in confidence daily. I will always remember holding Simone in my arms as a baby, then watching her take her first steps, and her first words. Little did I know that she would mutter another billion words over the next 30 years, and I would need to ask for time out to get a word in!!

As for those first steps, they became determined footsteps that continued through primary school, high school and university with numerous academic achievements. We have seen obstacles overcome, and accolades received, and witnessed remarkable growth and development in every aspect of Simone's life.

Through all these magical milestones, Simone has remained positive. She embodies a passion and zest for life that is infectious, and there are many of you here who have shared in those moments, which have been magical and many.

It has been a privilege to be a witness to the achievements of this amazing young lady who we are so proud is our daughter.

Simone, as you stand on the brink of a new chapter in your life, please know that we as your parents, are incredibly proud of you and we love you. When you were little, we always told you to reach for the moon, for if you miss you will land amongst the stars and be the brightest star, and you certainly are the brightest star darling daughter.

Tonight is your night, and we hope it will be a night that you will remember fondly, in the years ahead.

May you continue to walk, as sure-footed as you always have. May you remain as grounded as you have always been... and may you stay forever young in mind and spirit. Tonight, instead of counting candles, or tallying the years, contemplate the memories, the people who have enriched your life, and the experiences that have made you who you are.

And finally, when you blow out the last candle on your cake, remember that... Life holds no challenge, that you cannot handle...Happy 30th birthday baby, and lots of love to you from mum and me.

"Please join me in raising your glasses in a toast to Simone!!"

On another occasion, Simone decided to bring some fun to all her young cousins, their parents and her grandparents. So, Simone organised a fun afternoon during Christmas and hired a "Fire Engine" ride through the streets with a stopover to enjoy a spray of water from the fire engine.

The young cousins had a wonderful day and told Simone how thrilled they were to have such a "cool" fun day, asking what was next!

Speaking of Simone's many loves, nothing beats Simone's love of Christmas. She just adored "all things Christmas" and convinced her parents to enter the "Christmas Lights Competition every year. This became a 25-year tradition, and each year the family nominated a charity to which the proceeds of the busloads of visitors to the area would cheerfully donate.

The Christmas lights were a platform that catapulted Simone into a plane of pure enchantment and rapture where she delighted in the rich culture of all Christmas traditions. She wanted to share that experience with everyone both young and old and so as the season approached, she always embarked on a mammoth task with a super-abundance of enthusiasm.

Their house was often voted in the top five in the State. The display required an incredible amount of effort and would take Jennifer and Patrick close to a month to assemble, it brought so much joy and the time spent made it all worthwhile to see the thrilled faces of both the young and the not so young. Simone even bought matching Christmas shirts and nightwear to further brighten the occasion.

Simone used to contact all her friends to vote for her house in the Christmas Lights competition as she realised that her parents were having to pay the enormous electricity bill for the month of December, and she knew if they won the competition, it would assist her parents, as the prize for the competition was the electricity bill paid. Her parents marvelled at how hard Simone worked to contact her friends to vote, just to help them with the enormous electricity bill.

She also worked very hard to convince the attendees to help with the donations to the various charities, taking out the charity tins given by charities, even though there were times she had just come off dialysis, as she was aware how hard charities worked to raise funds and relied on community assistance to support the various causes.

Patrick and Jennifer recall that Simone believed all that was missing from their huge Christmas display was a Nativity Set and had been looking online for a while with no luck. However, on one occasion, while on one of their usual trips to Brisbane, Simone found a beautiful Nativity Set for sale and decided it was perfect, and so bought it to take back to Perth. However, it turned out quite a challenge to go and pick up the huge set, as it did not fit into the small hire car, so they had to sit with it on their laps and hope they did not get picked up by the traffic police.

Then came the challenge to take it up in the hotel lift, which was a very small lift as it was not the lobby lift but for carpark users only. Jennifer and Patrick recall how the hotel lift attendant gave the three of them strange looks, as they each had a figurine. Simone had baby Jesus, Jennifer had Mary, and Patrick had Joseph.

However, the challenge was hardest for Patrick, as Joseph was kneeling, and his kneeling leg was sticking right out, making it hard for Patrick to keep Joseph's leg safe from breaking. Patrick recalls how Jennifer and Simone were laughing hysterically, especially as Patrick was not at all impressed at having to manoeuvre Joseph in the small space in the lift. He was grumbling away about the ordeal he was experiencing, carrying Joseph. Jennifer recalls that she and Simone decided they would stir up the already grumbling Patrick and so Simone said "be careful dad, St. Joseph is not going to be impressed with you grumbling to carry him."

Patrick was trying hard not to damage the kneeling leg of Joseph. Patrick said it was even harder because Simone kept constantly saying "be careful dad, be careful dad." Patrick told Simone she was making him more nervous, than he already was, trying not to break Joseph's leg. While all this was going on, they did not realise that they were being watched.

They say they were so busy trying to keep the set safe that they did not notice that the lift attendant was looking at them very suspiciously, giving them strange looks, as he could not really see what they were carrying into the lift as the figurines were wrapped up in bubble wrap and so looked larger than the actual size.

Simone, saw the lift man looking at them strangely, and was worried about being reported to hotel management, so she explained it was for a Christmas display, hoping he would understand, but it got more hilarious, when he turned around and said "Lady, believe me I have seen people smuggling a lot of things into hotel rooms, but this one is definitely unique. I have never seen bubble wrapped people."

Patrick and Jennifer recall it was the first time they saw a worried look on Simone's face, as she went on again to reassure the lift attendant that they were really figurines and asked if he wanted to check it out, but he turned around and said, "Oh no, I am better off not knowing what you three are carrying." Jennifer and Patrick say they were happy to get out of the lift and into their room.

As soon as they got back home to Perth, Jennifer and Patrick recall how the excited Simone rang John from across the road. Simone asked if he would come and help her dad to build a home for baby Jesus, as she had just bought a huge Nativity Set and needed a manger. With Jennifer's help they turned it into a beautiful manger.

Not many people had a Nativity Scene, and so it was a real crowd pleaser as most people said for them Christmas Lights had lost its meaning of what Christmas is all about, but coming to Simone's display with the nativity scene portrayed the true meaning of Christmas.

Simone's immense love of Christmas soon had John involved as well in various aspects of showcasing the family's Christmas Display. John's family and friends, together with surrounding neighbours couldn't wait for the Christmas lights to go up each year. Sometimes, they would even ring Simone and ask her when the lights were going to go up. Patrick used to dread the reminder phone calls, as Simone would then beg him to start getting the lights out!!

When the display was ready, and the lights were turned on Simone was so very ecstatic. Jennifer and Patrick say how much they miss seeing the delighted face of their beautiful daughter. She was always so very ecstatic. Simone was absolutely delighted with every car and every bus load of people that came to visit her famous Christmas Lights, but she had a special place in her heart for the buses from the Aged Care Facility. Patrick recalls how one night she made him turn on all the lights back on again for the display when an Aged Care bus came later than the turn off time of 10.00 pm.

Patrick remembers Simone saying, "please dad you have to go and turn on the display for the oldies, remember they may not be here next Christmas" and of course dad said it made him feel so guilty, so he went and turned on the full display again, which was a huge task, but with the help of Jennifer he managed it. The family say it was a heartfelt inspiring moment when the oldies all cheered from the bus and called out a big "Thank You".

Simone would sit and design the whole display on a massive sheet of paper, making sure each light went according to her designed plan on paper, taking into consideration what would please children, adults and the very senior citizens who visited. She had a different colour theme each year. The year of "Frozen" Simone sought the help of her mum to make a beautiful carriage of lights for "Elsa and Anna" not realising it would turn out too popular and that the children would want to sit in the carriage with Elsa and Anna! A difficult situation for mum and dad, but very amusing for the fun-loving Simone!! However, that year Simone was absolutely thrilled when their house got voted the "Best Lights South of the River."

Simone spent a lot of money on her Christmas Lights. Her parents did not realise how generous their daughter really was all her life. Simone's life was not only focussed on sharing her advocacy skills but also her love of life by bringing joy and happiness to the local community.

Most people were totally unaware that the young enthusiastic girl who greeted them each night with a beaming smile, was fighting a battle to stay alive hooked up to a dialysis machine, yet she showed no sign of her ordeal but instead was thrilled each night to see how much joy her lights were bringing to the local community. It really took a lot of time, effort and dedication from Simone and her mum and dad as they had to finish a regime of dialysis for Simone, before the lights could go on, due to the use of the electricity.

In 2022, Simone did her usual Christmas message to the public advertising her beloved Christmas lights for public viewing as she had done for the last 25 years.

Sadly, this was Simone's last Christmas message to the public:

> *In 2022, this Christmas display will again be a fun and colourful display featuring more lights than one can count with over 5000 lights on the roof alone! SPECIAL FEATURES for 2022 include... A Merry Christmas Down Under Display featuring all of Australia's beloved wildlife including koalas, kangaroos, galahs and more. Inflatables of all types and sizes, a giant Golden Christmas Tree, a Golden Reindeer display, Santa's Disco with laser lights, a Photo Booth, where you can use your mobile to take photos to share the memories of your visit with your friends and family, and finally a Life Size Nativity Scene demonstrating the true meaning of*

Christmas. This display has something for the young and young at heart!!

Simone seemed unstoppable, embracing the famous phrase "Carpe Diem" seizing every moment of every day literally. Realising how precious life is, there was an urgency in her determination to fill 60 seconds of every minute of every day. Her supportive parents sometimes found it difficult to keep up with this pint-sized dynamo. Simone's drive to accomplish as much as possible was simply amazing and exhausting!

The Pandemic

The Covid-19 lockdown was particularly difficult for Simone, as she could not leave the house for approximately two years. Her immune system could not cope with the potential toll of contracting the virus. Her devoted parents continued with dialysis in their home.

At the time of the pandemic, Simone was only 38 years old and unable to visit friends or have visitors. She was fortunate to have a profession that allowed her to continue working remotely.

Always thinking of others, she would send her colleagues funny musical animations that she would edit by adding their faces to videos to cheer everyone up. Only a few people in the organisation ever knew the full extent of Simone's condition, and she preferred it that way.

To provide some much-needed fun and contrast to her captivity, Patrick, who is a gifted musician, would accompany Simone on the guitar and sing, while she played their favourite numbers on her keyboard, and sometimes on the piano, which she also loved. Simone loved her piano, as it was a special birthday gift from her dad for her 9th birthday. Simone was aware how hard her dad had worked with double shifts to make some extra money to buy her the piano. They would often have impromptu 'jam sessions' when they felt in the mood, while mum recorded them both for some added fun and laughter.

Simone was completely devastated when Covid-19 hit, and she was unable to attend the "Wild Cats" games and had to resort to watching it at home with her dad. At home, she still made the effort to dress up in full gear and insisted that dad did the same, and she endeavoured to create a "games" atmosphere with popcorn, coke, and frozen coke and made sure they had all the little 'Wildcats' merchandise to go with it.

Basically, Simone turned the family room into the RAC Arena; if she could not attend the game, she was determined to bring the game to her. Jennifer said the noise they both made really sounded like they both were at the RAC Arena. Jennifer and Patrick saw how very resilient to setbacks Simone really was, and that gave her the ability to find solutions, work around circumstances, and bounce back when things went wrong.

Simone had the ability to overcome the many sad and challenging times in her life, and she had the innate ability to turn every negative situation into a positive situation!! An amazing trait for a person whose life was filled with adversity.

Jennifer and Patrick believe their beloved daughter Simone's life, though filled with such heartache and adversity, was a preparation for greatness, as what this little butterfly achieved was simply amazing in her 40 years.

Also sharing a love of musical theatre, Patrick and Simone, before the pandemic used to perform for a private Theatre Company in various productions including "Fiddler on the Roof", "Snow White", and "Scrooge". So, when the pandemic hit, Simone was very disappointed that she was missing all the musicals that were coming to Perth during Covid-19. She would get out her DVDs and watch her favourites and keep herself happy enjoying her ardent love of the musicals of which she never tired. She also enjoyed her movies. She loved "Disney" and kept her favourite movie "Willie Wonka and the Chocolate Factory" close by, even though she had watched it over a hundred times. Simone was able to relate to this movie, as it conveyed the significance of humility, honesty, and kindness.

Unfortunately, Simone turned that wonderful milestone of 40 during Covid. All Simone's friends loved her birthday parties, and they always looked forward to her birthday. The birthday parties were always such a fun gathering. Simone was not going to let Covid-19 dampen her spirit of celebrating her 40th birthday, as she had a special fondness for parties. Birthdays, however, gave her the chance to have a party for her friends, and there was always a theme to highlight the event.

Due to Covid-19, as Simone could not meet her friends on her 40th birthday, she organised a "Zoom" party. However, her spirit of giving came to the fore, and she decided to organise a "keepsake memory box" to give to everybody. Being in lockdown, she requested her aunt to help buy all the boxes and ribbons for her and leave it at the door, which she was so thankful for.

Simone decorated all the "keepsake memory boxes" and put it outside and her lovely friends were excited to come and pick up their big "keepsake memory box" even though the weather was so bad. Each "keepsake memory box" besides being beautifully decorated was filled with items that gave the recipient a glimpse of her 40 years shared with them.

The "keepsake memory box" was tailored to suit each individual recipient and was filled with memorabilia of precious memories shared, and included sentimental treasured items, favourite foods, and photographs of their 40 years together. It was her way to show her friends and family how much she valued the precious memories and the connection shared. Even though it was a time-consuming endeavour to sort, fill and individually decorate each box, it was Simone's way to show the recipient how much she had enjoyed life's special moments with them; while celebrating the beautiful connection she had shared with them.

Jennifer and Patrick recall it broke their hearts to see Simone finish a rigorous dialysis session, and then painstakingly work on those "keepsake memory boxes" especially as Simone was such a perfectionist, so it took a long time to assemble.

Jennifer and Patrick say they are reminded how diligently Simone worked to source each item on-line and recall the item that stood out was a set of plastic dentures arriving by post, which was to go in her nanny's "keepsake memory box" just to tease her nanny!! Simone always had to incorporate that element of fun in all her ventures.

On the day of her 40th birthday, Simone was happily surprised to wake up to her front garden filled with "Winnie the Pooh" ornaments from her friends, and a massive "Happy 40th Birthday Simone" sign given by her aunt and uncle.

It is sad that Covid-19 also destroyed the fun-loving Simone from catching up with her friends whilst driving her red sports car, which was a passion that reflected her daring race against time to get things done.

A Race Against Time To Survive...

Manoeuvring the storms of life was the epitome of Simone's life, and for Jennifer and Patrick they say life felt like they were surrounded by a fierce battle in the storm, with no bridge to cross. It was only heartache at each twist and turn in the road to help them navigate the trials and tribulations of trying to give their child a normal life...one would think it wasn't a big ask but it wasn't how the pages of Simone's life panned out, as depicted below.

Born with a single poorly functioning kidney, which gave up in 1991, Simone had to go on dialysis at the age of 9 years. She continued dialysis during the night, so she could continue with a normal school life. Simone was put on the Transplant Waiting List, and after three years on the list, received a cadaver kidney.

In 1993, Simone was given a kidney transplant while in the children's hospital, only to discover not long after that it was a poorly matched kidney. Shortly before being moved to the adult hospital, Simone was given a medication that propelled her kidney into rejection. Simone was then told the medication had caused the rejection of the kidney. Later, Simone was transferred to the adult hospital.

In 2009, due to the rejection, Simone had to go back onto dialysis again. Simone continued dialysis while still being actively involved in raising the profile of organ donation through her organisation that she founded the Organ Donation and Transplant Foundation of W.A.

Simone worked tirelessly raising the profile of organ donation even whilst working and having to be hooked up to a machine three times a week to survive. However, nothing daunted this little human dynamo who some nick-named "ever ready battery."

In 2011, after waiting three years on dialysis, Jennifer approached Simone's specialist at that time and asked for Simone to be put on the Transplant Waiting List. He agreed with conditions.

Jennifer was told that he could not put Simone on the Transplant Waiting List unless she had a nephrectomy due to having a kidney stone. Jennifer said she was apprehensive for Simone to have the nephrectomy operation and asked the specialist if they could take out the old kidney with the stone at the time when they give her a new kidney transplant, but the specialist told Jennifer "No Nephrectomy No List".

So, in 2011, Simone's desperation for a kidney transplant, saw her sign up for the nephrectomy operation, which turned out a disaster. The nephrectomy did not succeed and Simone had to be rushed back into the operating theatre as she was bleeding internally.

Jennifer and Patrick said they only found out Simone was bleeding internally when she was sent to dialysis following the nephrectomy. While Simone was at dialysis after the nephrectomy, Jennifer said, she heard Patrick screaming to the nurse to stop the dialysis machine, as Patrick saw Simone's body slumped in the chair. Simone was bleeding internally, and she had to be rushed back into theatre to stop the bleeding.

Jennifer and Patrick's world fell apart, when one of the nurses told them every minute counted so not to delay them, because they were trying to kiss their daughter before she went into theatre like all people do. It was only then that Jennifer and Patrick began to panic when they realised how critical the situation was when they saw the theatre staff rushing Simone down the corridor to the operating theatre.

Simone was rushed back into theatre to stop the bleeding and Simone's friend Becky had just come to visit and was horrified to see Simone being rushed down the corridor. Jennifer and Patrick are so thankful that Becky came. Becky sat in the middle of them and they all three prayed for Simone to come out safely.

However, worse was still to come and Patrick, Jennifer and Becky were in for another horrific shock, when Simone was wheeled out on a ventilator.

Simone had to be given blood transfusions. The blood transfusion put Simone in the "highly sensitised" category making the "Authorities' decide that giving "Simone a kidney would be a waste to society." A statement that still haunts and hurts the family till today as parents of such a brilliant young person like Simone. A statement that would hurt and destroy any parent.

Jennifer and Patrick say that even now the statement still destroys them as their daughter was precious to them like any child is to a parent, and suggesting saving her life was a waste to society was shocking and appalling. One can only imagine the pain and anguish of that statement on Simone's parents, describing their cherished daughter, especially given Simone's immense contributions to society. The many awards and accolades are a testament to that.

Most people are aware that Simone dedicated her life and all her spare time raising the profile of organ and tissue donation, and was a well-known tireless community worker, who worked relentlessly doing her charity work even though she was on dialysis three times a week.

This little pocket rocket was heavily involved in championing many causes, giving her time freely despite the regime of dialysis, and so it is no wonder that the statement was so hurtful to the parents of such a dedicated community worker. Jennifer says they waited in the wings for six years hoping to find Simone a live donor, but unfortunately there was no match to be found.

Not long after that decision was made by the Perth medical transplant fraternity not to give Simone a kidney, hope came in the form of a doctor friend of Simone's who willingly referred her to a doctor in Queensland, who was prepared to put Simone on the Transplant Waiting List, but it came at a price, as the family would have to reside in Queensland to qualify.

The family knew that time was of the essence, if they were to save Simone's life, and so in desperation, the family gave up their jobs, took out their superannuation, and headed to Queensland, as they knew they had to grab this lifeline hoping, to save their daughters life.

Ironically, this was the same National Transplant List for the whole country, but this family was given no choice but to leave their home state, and everything familiar to go to Queensland to get on that same National Transplant List. This was an unnecessary stress that was put on a loving family in crisis. The forced interstate move crippled the family financially, and the timing for their arrival in Queensland couldn't have been worse as employment prospects were next to impossible.

Simone contacted a friend of a friend to get them an apartment and Simone ordered two beds online. Simone and her family took the empty apartment close to the hospital arranged through that friend. All they had in the apartment were the two beds and no other furniture. A kidney health worker friend of Simone's picked the family up from the airport and brought with her a few utensils, a toaster and some cutlery held in an Esky. Jennifer and Patrick gave that Esky to Simone to sit on, while they sat on the floor as they had no furniture, only the two beds.

Furnishing their little apartment proved to be a challenge, as when they went to the furniture sales room to buy furniture, they were told they would have to wait weeks for the furniture to be delivered. No one was willing to sell them display furniture, and even purchasing second-hand furniture wasn't possible because the family didn't have a car.

Jennifer and Patrick said that when Simone was put on the "Transplant Waiting List" in Queensland within six weeks of arriving, in the northern state, all the despair and anguish of leaving their home, family, and friends vanished at the news, as well as the agony of sitting on the floor!

Everything happens for a reason, they say, and that reason caused a shift and transformation. The ever-close bond between Simone and her parents became even stronger as they pulled together to battle against all odds. Jennifer and Patrick said that Simone changed during their time in Queensland. Although we will never know for sure, they saw a renewed optimism in Simone, probably due to the prospect of a new kidney and a new life.

Simone was invited to speak for the Centre of Stories program at ABC while in Queensland. Below is an extract of Simone's speech.

My parents knew that I would need a kidney transplant after I was born with one kidney which didn't function very well, and completely failed when I was nine years old, and so from a very young age I went on dialysis and was on the waiting list for my first kidney transplant, which I was fortunate enough to receive when I was 11 years old, from a deceased donor.

My name is Simone McMahon. I am the Founder and Chief Executive Officer of the Organ Donation and Transplant Foundation of W.A. My childhood, as a result of waiting for a transplant, was very different to your average 9 or 10 years old going for sporting carnivals or going out for sleepovers with their friends. I obviously had to be home every night so I could be hooked up to my dialysis machine over night for basically 11 hours, and this went on for almost 3 years of my childhood, while I waited for the telephone call to come for a transplant.

It was quite challenging going to school. I was very unwell at the time, and making a full week at school was practically impossible. I was getting help with my maths homework when at 9.20 pm the phone rang, and it was the doctor saying a kidney was available.

When I woke up in the intensive care, the first words that came out of my mouth were, I don't feel tired anymore. That was the first thing that hit me, despite coming out of anaesthetic and major surgery, it was still a tremendous difference that you could feel almost immediately.

I've never really had that opportunity to meet the family of the donor that did give me that "Gift of Life". I certainly know the difference that decision made to my life, and the things that I have been able to achieve as a result of that decision, so I think it is certainly a bond that you feel within you, even though you personally don't know the family.

I pretty much started volunteering almost immediately after my first transplant. I was 11 at that time, and the very first thing was speaking publicly at the Penguin Speak Up Awards, where I spoke about organ and tissue donation and, interestingly enough, my speech was called recycling. At that time in the early 90s, everyone was talking about recycling the cans, the bottles and so forth.

Many of the adjudicators looked at me like not another one, but of course mine was a very different recycling speech as I spoke about recycling so to speak, about organs through organ donation and the "Gift of Life" that organ donation can achieve. I was very fortunate to be selected right through to the grand finals, and from that, doors opened to speak more publicly about my experience, and raise awareness about organ and tissue donation.

The Churchill Fellowship provided a platform for me to take the organ donation advocacy to the next level and enabled me to travel to the US, UK and Spain, and work with several organisations to really enlighten myself and experience organ and tissue donation programs at a completely new level.

I have always been a West Australian, and I found there were many organisations and community organisations that promoted organ and tissue donation at a National Body, and I have been involved in many of them. There was nothing actually set up that catered only to West Australians.

Western Australia has a lot of issues that is only unique to W.A. that impacts only organ and tissue donation, and one of the main issues we have in W.A. where the other States don't necessarily have to the extent of W.A. is obviously the distance. Organ donation specifically has very limited criteria that makes donation possible, and in fact, only 1% of all people that die, die in a situation where they can actually be organ donors. W.A. is such a vast area, and so, it impacts significantly the location on where a person is, and whether they will be able to be a donor or not, and that is something that doesn't necessarily impact on some other states in Australia.

My kidney transplant I had in 1993 functioned well enough without dialysis, for me to survive without dialysis for a full 16-year period, which was wonderful, but unfortunately after the16-year period my kidney function did start to decline. I did have to return to dialysis to keep me alive, so for the past 7 years I have essentially been on dialysis waiting for a second kidney transplant, that's where I am at the moment waiting for the phone call to ring to give me another second chance at life.

A second transplant is always more complex than the first transplant for a number of medical reasons, as there is a very strict criteria to receive a transplant, and that's whether it is a 1st, 2nd or 3rd. The health professionals in W.A. declined me from being a suitable candidate on the donor list, which is a deceased donor list in W.A.

Fortunately, Queensland was willing to consider me as a suitable candidate to be listed. We all three, my parents, and myself, left family, jobs, everything behind to live in a state where we didn't know anyone. We have not lived outside W.A. before, so it was very new, and a big step, with big challenges, but sometimes you have to do what you have to do, to give yourself a second chance at life, and it was my only hope, and I was very fortunate that Queensland was prepared to consider me for a transplant on the deceased donor list.

Perth was only prepared to accept me for a transplant with a live donor, and all the family members that did come forward to be tested were unfortunately not matches. We arrived to a very empty two-bedroom apartment, just outside Brisbane and we've been living there while we wait for the transplant to happen. I have dialysis set up in my bedroom, and I have dialysis 3-4 times a week for approximately 3 to 4 hours. The machine is obviously what keeps me alive, it cleans out my blood until I can find a new kidney to do that job.

Financially, it has been a struggle to move here, and it's one expensive journey to leave Western Australia. The call for a transplant could come tomorrow, the call could come in five years' time, obviously it's the unknown that is challenging because you are waiting for that phone to ring, and you are away from family, friends, you are in a place where you don't know how long you have to make that your home.

The deceased donor list is a National List, and I think generally speaking if one state would be willing to accept you as a suitable candidate, then the criteria should be pretty much the same across the board, across all states. I don't think anyone should be put into a situation where they have to leave their home, leave their loved *ones just to be able to be given the opportunity to essentially just survive.*

During the period in Queensland, when Jennifer and Patrick were constantly worried, their lively daughter was able to keep their spirits up. The family didn't have any moral support from anyone, as they did not know anyone in Queensland and relied on each other for strength.

Nothing ever seemed to daunt Simone, and her sunny outlook always enabled her to make the best of a bad situation. Simone sourced as many free events as possible around the city to keep the family's spirits high. Jennifer recalls that Simone even took them to the local growers' markets every Sunday to buy cheap vegetables, whilst also exploring the stalls. The family hadn't attended as many free events in Perth, so it was quite an adventure! Simone loved the thrill of each outing and experience.

Then came a day while the family was still in Queensland, the zesty Simone told her parents that she needed a hobby to help her relax. She had read that painting was ideal for relaxation, so off she went to the local artist store and came home with a box full of paints in one hand and a stack of canvases under the other arm.

As she walked in, her dad Patrick, true to form, teased and said, "Here comes our little Picasso". With her usual gusto, Simone mastered commercial art and sold her paintings at the local markets! I think her dad was slowly learning not to underestimate his spirited daughter, as time and time again she excelled in everything she undertook and proved that she could do whatever she made up her mind to do.

Jennifer and Patrick soon realised the breadth and depth of skills their diminutive daughter possessed, as even they were completely blown away by Simone's next venture. The forced move to Queensland had severely impacted the family's finances, and it is true to say that just as her parents were willing to do anything to save their child, Simone's natural entrepreneurial mind was always mulling over ideas, to assist with the family's finances.

Whilst in Queensland, Simone happened to visit a "Wellness Fair" and observed that the crystal healing stall was doing very well. She approached the stall holder and asked the lady for her assistance in becoming a crystal healer. Within a month, she had completed an intense course, and she was off and running as a crystal healer! Her parents were in awe of Simone's resourcefulness and remember how they helped Simone set up for her first "Wellness Fair'.

Patrick had a new name again for Simone in this new venture, he couldn't resist calling Simone "Billie Crystal". Simone showed mock annoyance, but father and daughter had this special bond that even if she got annoyed, he would somehow soon have her laughing at the often-weird names he came up with for all her little ventures. With this latest venture, Patrick wasn't entirely convinced, that Simone could pull it off, but as always was willing to support her.

He sat on the sidelines watching with amusement, and very soon realised that Simone was proving him wrong yet again! Simone, using her artistic skills had dressed up her stall so well that it had immediate appeal to the passers-by. It wasn't long before Simone had a queue of customers.

Patrick well remembers her casting him a mischievous glance now and then, obviously quite pleased with herself. When she came home, she showed her dad her takings for the day and said, "What have you got to say for yourself - "Doubting Thomas?' Jennifer remembers telling Patrick, it was time that he acknowledged Simone was going to outwit him every time, but Patrick enjoyed giving Simone different names every time she took up a new venture.

Her next course was Palmistry, and she undertook this interesting course so that she could provide another addition to the services offered at the Wellness Fairs. Simone was very excited about doing courses, and whilst she was searching for a job in Queensland, she even tried to enrol Patrick in a course.

Simone believed that Patrick had 'healing hands' and had an amazing ability to massage out knots, so it seemed logical to her to enrol him in an online "Masseur" course!! Jennifer said it was the one time she laughingly recalls when Patrick put his foot down and said, 'No way!' He announced, 'I am not like that 'Sven' character in the TV advertisement".

Patrick was so shocked at even the thought of this activity. Simone burst out laughing and used this name to tease him when she wanted to irritate her dad by playfully calling him 'Sven.'

Simone had Patrick wrapped around her little finger, as most daughters can do with their dads. Theirs was a beautiful relationship. Patrick was outnumbered, living in the house with two women but he enjoyed every minute of it.

The family roughed it out for two whole years, desperately hoping for that phone call that all transplant patients wait for, but sadly it never happened. Unfortunately, not being able to attain employment crippled the family financially, and it became increasingly apparent that the family couldn't carry on waiting for the transplant whilst living in Queensland, as it was draining their finances and making it impossible for them to continue to live there.

Jennifer and Patrick said it destroyed them to break the news to Simone, that they would have to return to Perth. The money was running out, and they simply had no other option available. As parents, they felt the lifeboat that was to carry their child through the storm of life on dialysis had sunk, and they were now left without that lifeline that they had pinned their hopes on.

As parents, they felt it was the hardest thing they had to do. They are continually haunted with thoughts of "what if" contemplating a very different scenario that if their money had not run out would their darling daughter Simone still be here.

Jennifer and Patrick said it totally devastated them to inform their beautiful daughter that their money was dwindling, and the rent was getting harder to pay. As parents, they said that it was the hardest thing they had to do to tell Simone, their beautiful daughter, that they had to return to Perth.

Jennifer says she still remembers looking into Simone's beautiful brown eyes and says she is still haunted with a feeling of utter guilt, that because of a lack of money, they had to return to Perth and remembers how she and Patrick found it so hard to look at Simone's face and inform her that sadly they could not stay any longer in Queensland. They are continually haunted with the thoughts of the "what ifs" contemplating a very different scenario, that if their money had not run out, would their darling daughter Simone still be here. The emotional trauma of these parents remains, and still haunts them that their lack of money could have cost them their beautiful daughter's life.

Jennifer and Patrick say the doctor in Queensland very kindly said that they could return once they were able to save enough money, and the family could carry on from where they left off. The kind words of the doctor were well-meaning, and meant to reassure the family, but returning to Perth, settling, and seeking employment was once again a huge undertaking.

However, on their return after their traumatic exit from Queensland, they were forced to navigate through another emotional challenge. It looked like life was not meant to be easy for these loving parents, whose only one wish was to give their daughter a chance at a normal life, and not a life hooked up to a machine to survive, as they knew they were blessed with a daughter that was born to be a beacon of light to those without the ability to defend themselves.

On their return to Perth, Jennifer received a phone call from the Renal Department telling her that the Department was going to remove Simone's dialysis machine. They were claiming that

Jennifer and Patrick were not following the right "technique" for conducting her dialysis.

Jennifer was stunned that the Renal Department could make such a claim, and asked how they had arrived at that decision, considering the family had been conducting dialysis successfully for nine years. Earlier in that same month, Simone had brought to the notice of the Renal Department team that the dialysis lines for the machine were faulty and had leaked.

The family understood that all the other states of Australia had changed dialysis lines, but Perth did not follow the other states and had no intention of changing the lines. The reason for this difference between the states is that in Perth, dialysis is run by a private company.

Life became another challenge for this family with a fight to keep the dialysis machine at home. The family was not going to hand back the vitally needed machine without a fight, as having the machine at home enabled Simone, Jennifer and Patrick to have full-time jobs as well as live as normal a life as one can, being on a regime of dialysis three times a week. So the Dialysis Department cut off the dialysis supplies and had instructed the delivery man not to deliver the much-needed supplies.

The delivery was to be on a Friday and Jennifer said that it was either through luck or divine intervention, that the delivery man did not want the responsibility of holding the supplies over the weekend, so he left the supplies at the house for Simone. It was one month of supplies and that bought Jennifer and Patrick some time to seek legal advice.

The family had to spring into action quickly, if it was possible to keep the dialysis machine at home. Jennifer phoned a prominent lawyer named John Hammond who was utterly shocked and furious to hear of Simone's plight at the life and death situation the family found themselves in.

John Hammond immediately came to the family's aid, together with Pip Brennan, who was a part of The Health Consumer Council at that time, and together they worked tirelessly to sort out this life-saving issue.

John Hammond and Simone, who were both lawyers, joined forces and worked furiously to overturn the Renal Department's decision within that very short time frame. Assisted by Pip Brennan of The Health Consumer Council, they were able to put the case forward that Simone needed home dialysis as this enabled her to work from home.

Unfortunately, the Dialysis and Renal Unit would not back down. They then insisted that Jennifer and Patrick had to pass a 'Technique Test.' So, three nurses and a nephrologist were sent to the house and the dialysis supplies were kept in the nurses' car, even though it was a hot December day, until the parents passed the 'Test.' These loving parents were put under enormous stress, as they realised what was at stake for their daughter.

Four people scrutinised their "technique" as they hooked Simone onto dialysis. Jennifer and Patrick's nervousness had nothing to do with their own competence. After all, they had been carrying out this procedure for nine years. It was their mistrust of the Dialysis and Renal Unit that they could 'discover something wrong' and take away their daughter's life-giving machine on a whim that worried them most of all. They passed the test and then the supplies were handed over.

The parents say that their beautiful daughter Simone kept reassuring them that she had implicit faith in them, that they had nothing to worry about and that they should not be intimidated.

Simone gave them the courage to undergo the 'Test' and as they looked at their precious daughter's face, they say Simone must have seen their distress and willed them to be strong throughout the ordeal.

It was Christmas Eve, and instead of being a time of joy and peace for the family, they were locked into a fight to keep the dialysis machine at home, that helped Simone to lead as normal a life as possible given the restrictions of dialysis, and it was what enabled her to be fulfilled and productive in her many roles.

Jennifer and Patrick say that they remain forever grateful to John Hammond for his legal representation and Pip Brennan, formerly of the Health Consumer Council, as without their kind assistance they would not have won that intolerable fight to keep the dialysis machine, and the return of the supplies. The invaluable assistance of John Hammond and Pip Brennan enabled Simone to continue her legal work, her advocacy work, and her charity work volunteering, and all those roles were time consuming and being on home dialysis enabled her to accomplish all those roles.

The Fight and Flight of a Butterfly

A fleeting butterfly that flew in for a brief time and escaped the cocoon to make a mark on the world...

Simone's life was fleeting... here one moment gone the next like a butterfly that flew in, unfolded its wings and like a butterfly's incredible struggle for transformation, she wove her existence striving to capture a life filled with fun, laughter, whilst becoming a symbol of hope to the vulnerable.

Like a butterfly struggles, Simone's struggles to live eventually overtook her and her battle to survive against all the insurmountable odds was lost. It was a fight well fought but sadly this time the battle to survive could not be won and she was unable to finish the race... the world lost a shining star and heaven gained an angel.

This beautiful butterfly had to leave her cocoon of her life here on earth and she winged her way to heaven leaving a lasting legacy to treasure.

It was a priceless legacy of a life well lived, of service to others and cherished moments of love, laughter and pride for those who loved her to treasure forever.

Simone had a love of quotes by Sir Winston Churchill... her favourite...

"We make a living by what we get, but we make a life by what we give."

Simone gave her best to society and unquestionably left an indelible mark on all who knew her.

A Treasury of Tributes

Simone, your life was a blessing,
Your memory a treasure,
You are loved beyond words,
And missed beyond measure.

The following tributes portray the fabric of your life, from so many people from different walks of life, who have experienced your determination, your courage, your zest for life and your selflessness to alleviate suffering...

Simone, you remained an indomitable warrior, fierce, strong and immune to adversity, who fought the good fight right to the end without a thought of yourself. You were born to be a legend...

Jennifer and Patrick McMahon

Simone's Parents

Our darling Simone, you were the best gift we ever received, and our biggest achievement. In the pages of our life, you were our most beautiful chapter.

From the moment you were born, you captivated our hearts. You became every breath we took, and our whole world was wrapped up in you.

Our love for you transcends time and space, and it's unquantifiable. You illuminated our darkest days and provided that radiant beam to help us overcome the insurmountable challenges that the three of us encountered. The challenges came fast and furious, but our family was a circle of strength and love, and your presence added more joy and love, and every crisis faced made the circle of love stronger.

Your father and I believe the strength of our family was like the strength of an army, and you, our darling daughter, were our little "General." We enjoyed your amusing little "commands" and most people knew that you had your father under your command. He was also your little "genie" granting you all your wishes, as he was totally and utterly "bewitched" from the day you were born, when he first held you in his arms.

Whereas you and me, my darling Simone, had a special bond that spanned the years. A sense of trust that no one could break, and a warmth and caring that stood the test of time, of all the challenges we faced together. I feel so very blessed and fortunate to have been your mother, except I still cannot forgive myself, my darling, for not being able to save your life. I feel like half of my heart is missing, as I miss you beyond measure, and the pain never ceases. Each day remains a struggle, and my heartache remains unbearable. Sorrow has become my shroud. Your leaving consumes my being, and I wish I could turn back time. The chaos of grief is mired in misery.

You were the most generous daughter, always giving us presents, and the immense joy of giving was obvious in your beautiful face whenever you came home with something to brighten our day! The best and most memorable gift was when you walked in the door one day and gave us an envelope and said excitedly, 'open it up' and when we opened it, we were engulfed with a sense of utter euphoric happiness.

In the envelope were three round-the-world tickets. We realised how hard you must have saved to get those tickets for the three of us, as you had only just started working and between the tears and the hugs, we realised how blessed we were to have a wonderful daughter like you. Simone, you our darling daughter, brought nothing but profound, immeasurable joy to our life, and captured our world, with an intense love that bound us in a unique bond together.

It was not only us, your parents, that you were generous to. From the young age of 14, from your first pay, you came home with presents for all your cousins and your grandparents. You were also the organiser of all outings for the family, and later for your friends who you managed to convince to share in your fun and sometimes crazy outings. We are so glad that you made the most of your short life, darling.

You were our pride and joy darling Simone, as when we see all your achievements and accomplishments it blows our minds away, how someone who had so many challenges to face could accomplish so much in her life, in the face of such great adversity. You were one in a million and definitely "Simply the Best".

We as your parents feel heartbroken and cheated, that you were not given a second transplant because the authorities felt "giving you a transplant would be a waste to society." If there was anyone, who has done so much for society, it was you. Your awards are testimony and acknowledgment of that fact. The words of the "Authorities" constantly haunts and hurts us. We had to go through sheer emotional distress to try and save your life leaving our home to go to Queensland, which was the hardest and challenging time for all of us, but as your parents we blame ourselves that our financial status played a part in not being able to save your life.

Unfortunately, life for the three of us was always trying to overcome insurmountable challenges. Our life seemed to be always filled with stormy weather throughout. However, you saw a silver lining in every dark cloud and brightened every day from the moment you woke up in the morning, and the first words were "Dad". Your father is heartbroken that he cannot hear those words each morning, and I am heartbroken that I cannot hear your voice calling me "Mum" and if I didn't answer, you would call out "Jen" and I would answer, and you would joke and say, "Well that got your attention. didn't it, Jen." We really miss all that baby. We sit here heartbroken and wonder how we are going to face another new day without you.

When you left, it broke us into a million pieces. The pain of losing you is indescribable, but the unique bond of love that the three of us shared, and which no one else will ever understand, is what sustains us in our darkest days.

We hide our tears when we hear your name, because the pain in our hearts is still the same. You remain in our thoughts every day, and we wish we could have the chance to see your face one more time or hear your voice one more time.

Although we smile and seem carefree, no one knows how our heart aches for you. How do we stop this ache in our heart? The tears still flow incessantly, and if only tears could build a stairway and memories a lane, we would walk straight up to heaven and bring you home again.

As each day dawns, we feel the light has gone out of our lives, darling daughter, but our love for you and the memories we shared still burns brightly like a candle. Simone, our darling daughter, you were our "Special Angel" sent from heaven above. We know even though you are now in heaven that you have not left us and are now watching over us. The song "Special Angel" was our song for you from the day you were born, and now every time we hear it, we realise how true the words are. You will never be forgotten; we pledge to you each day a hollowed place within our hearts, where you will always stay.

Yours was a life filled with so much hope, but that life was cut short because a kidney transplant was unavailable for you. Thirteen long years you fought to survive, and you fought all the way darling. It was a fight to survive against the greatest adversity. We fought with you too, but the ache in our heart remains unbearable. There are days where we question ourselves, as we feel like we did not do enough, and wonder if there was any more, we could have done.

Our house feels empty. The days are dark and lonely, and our hearts are woven in sorrow and darkness. It's only your memory that lights our way and helps us through another day. The saying "grief has no road map" is so true. As time marches on we are consoled with the thought our hearts were linked with such a strong love and the knowledge of that is in some way comforting.

We know how you loved John Farnham and when we hear "Baby without you" the words say it all for us.

"Sitting here in my lonely room, feeling all alone and blue, and I just can't seem to make it baby without you."

Till that link in our chain of love is joined again baby, we remain forever, your very shattered Mum and Dad.

Rita Woods

Simone's Maternal Grandmother

Simone... my most precious, most unforgettable character

It was a winter's morn and dawn's early light bathed the city of Perth in its bright glow, when a beautiful little baby was placed in my arms. Oh, how thrilled I was to see this fairy-like babe with a pretty heart-shaped face framed in a wealth of lustrous black hair... this was Simone and she belonged to me, my precious first grandchild.

As I gazed into her little face, I knew my life would never be the same, for she captured my heart and my very being.

Simone at two years, exuded brilliance. Not wanting to waste this talent, I started teaching her. When she started school, I was summoned to the principal's office and was reprimanded for teaching her. I was bewildered. Shouldn't they be proud of her? I thought, but the principal said she would have to build a special classroom and engage a special teacher for her. She said when the teacher chose a topic and started teaching, little Simone would stand up and take over from the teacher for, she knew too much, so I was banned from teaching her for several years.

Not wanting to waste the talent of this exceptional child, I got my daughter Jennifer, who is Simone's mum, to buy her a little keyboard, which we couldn't really afford at the time, so I could teach her to play the piano. Simone was only 6 years old when I entered her in a Talent Quest organised by the new shopping centre. Simone's mum was apprehensive that Simone would have to compete with adults.

Come Talent Quest morning little Simone, dressed in a pretty pink dress, walked onto the stage, and sat at the old second-hand keyboard, but she played like a professional and walked away with the prize, much to the surprise of the adult competitors.

What I admired most in Simone was that she was always humble and unassuming. Accolades flooded her early life, and later into young adulthood, but Simone remained the sweet, humble person that she was. I introduced her to the "Musicals", and she was hooked!! The two of us went to almost every one of them that came to Perth. We enjoyed those times together, every single moment – a beautiful togetherness.

As an adult, despite insurmountable health issues, she soldiered on, trying to raise the profile of organ and tissue donation with the opening of her own Foundation – The Organ Donation and Transplant Foundation of W.A. realising the need to help those awaiting transplants. Simone somehow achieved the impossible, granting wishes for children, while she volunteered tirelessly at the Starlight Children's Foundation as a wish granter. Simone really excelled in this, as she was always thrilled to see the joy she brought. I was so proud that this marvellous, glorious personage who was my granddaughter created so much joy because of her arduous efforts, whilst neglecting her own great needs.

I recall one most amazing project of Simone's. She decided to organise a Sunday in Perth to promote Organ Donation, which was her most cherished wish. She visited every religious denomination, every church, temple, synagogue, Gurdwara, and even the smallest religious hub throughout Perth with an information package and a candle to burn on a particular day.

Even though it took a long time to traverse the whole of Perth, she achieved this mammoth task. This beautiful petite "Angel of Mercy" pleaded with so much passion and fire for the need for everyone to join in prayer. So, on a special Sunday, various denominations lit the candle and the hearts of worshippers of all creeds in Perth beat as 'One' on that special day. What a super achievement!!

Sadly, she pursued the gift of organ donation for others yet neglected her own great need. All she strove for was to alleviate the suffering of as many as she could. Is it a small wonder that I always told her that 'she was my pride and joy?'

Simone knew how I longed to travel, and my dream was to visit Venice and float down the Grand Canal in a Gondola. However, circumstances prevented all that, but when I heard that Venice was on Simone's itinerary, I was extremely happy. Whenever Simone's trip commenced, she would phone me describing the city she was visiting, its environs and its people enabling me to be a part of those faraway places, as she knew how much I had wanted to travel.

In the early hours one morning I was woken with an excited Simone calling me here in Perth "Nannie I have a lovely surprise for you, listen!" I then heard a male voice start to sing "Santa Lucia", and I heard her say "I am floating down the Grand Canal in Venice, and I've got the Gondolier to sing just for you". The moment the first verse ended, all the occupants of the Gondola joined in the refrain followed by much cheering and laughter. It was indeed a veritable feast for my ears hearing those glorious rich voices raised in song, and all just for "ME". I could never hope to visit Venice, so my darling Simone brought Venice to me! This interlude was a harmony of pure magic, and one I will cherish all my life. I am 88 years old now, and it still is a delightful vivid memory.

Simone personified "Carpe Diem" she never squandered a single moment, never let it pass by unheeded but was always reaching out to grasp it with both hands, and in doing so always attaining success, in this case she brought her grand-mother inexplicable joy.

That was "My Simone", my precious most unforgettable character!!

Simone's life was indeed a 'many splendoured thing', a great inspiration, like a little pebble when thrown into a pool that creates a little ripple that goes on to create ripple after ripple encompassing the whole pool. Simone was a force for good with the constructive influence she brought to bear on the lives that needed organs to survive... to quote the great poet James Shirley, 'Only the actions of the just smell sweet and blossom in the dust'.

Simone my darling, your actions will live on forever more, and I will remain your ever so proud Nanny.

Lesley-Ann Woods

My Godmother and Cousin, Simone McMahon

Simone has always been one of the biggest role models in my life. She was my godmother and cousin, and one of the people that helped mould me into the person I am today. I never thought the day would come, where I had to write about her in the past tense, but here I am.

There is no other word that can describe her work, her passions and everything that encompassed her than "Impeccable". Simone was impeccable, she was flawless. Though she had one of the hardest lives than most people ever would have, she pushed through it and achieved more than the average person. She was the most perfect role model that someone like me could look up to.

My earliest memories of Simone are when I was four. It was Christmas Day and Boo (Uncle Patrick) was Santa. The whole family was there including Simone. She was dressed in green, and her hair was the most beautiful thing I had seen at the time. I remember taking a photo with her, and then going along to play with my little mechanical car that I got for Christmas.

It was also at the age of four that Simone gave me my most favourite memory of all time. I never knew how she did it, but she ended up getting a fire truck, for the whole family. Being together with her and all the cousins on that fire truck, will always be the best memory of mine. Simone always managed to make everyone around her happy. She has contributed to some of the best memories in my childhood and I am forever grateful for that, and it pains me that I can never thank her for creating these memories and being a part of them.

When I was little older and able to comprehend art more, Simone was able to relay her passion for musical theatre onto me. We saw "Wicked" at the Crown Theatre. Though some memories have faded, I still remember seeing the Wicked Witch Elphaba sing Defying Gravity while she was elevated high above the stage floor, and I just remember looking over at Simone who was just awe struck taking in the incredible performance.

From that moment on that song has always stuck with me and my passion for musical theatre has just grown. She was so in love with musical theatre that her bedroom was also all musical theatre based.

Her pink room had all the posters of all her favourite shows and her closet had the most. My dream is to be like her and see Broadway Musicals and West End Musicals, and just experience the incredible musicals.

It is not an understatement when I say that she ignited her passion for art in me. She introduced me to my first ballet school, The Stage Key Company, where my interest in Ballet was nurtured to eventually become a passion and lifestyle of mine. I eventually went to a ballet specialist high school where I trained part-time at school and truly fell in love with the arts and everything that it had to offer. It was at this high school that she also helped me present her "Recycling Organs" speech at a speech competition. I was so happy to spend time with her and recreate her old speech. It was such an honour to speak to help her spread the word about organ donation and I only wish I could've gotten further in the competition to continue to spread awareness, but either way, I know she was proud of me.

After that competition Simone gave me the tips for acknowledging my nerves and not letting them get the better of me, she told me to look everyone in the eyes like I was having a conversation with them so I wouldn't be scared to speak in front of crowds. She let me hone in on my public speaking skills so that over time it went from something I was afraid of doing to something I would get the highest marks for in any assignment.

If I told every memory, it would take hours and pages and either way, I think I would like to keep some memories of hers close to my heart.

Simone was such a significant part of my life that every memory that I still have of her is a treasured gift that I will never take for granted.

Throughout my whole life, I always aspired to be like Simone. I still admire her so much. Every little kid has their heroes and who they want to be like when are growing up, it's always celebrities or musicians. Mine was Simone. She's been such an inspiration to me my whole life. She's fought for people disadvantaged in life like herself and studied to understand how to make a change and use the system of law to her advantage. She helped people, and I watched from afar in awe of her. I can only wish to be half of what she is. She will always be my inspiration; I will forever be grateful to have had her in my life. Simone was one of the kindest, smartest and most caring individuals I have ever known.

I wish I could've spoken to her more towards the end, and told her how much I appreciated her, love her, and thank her for everything she has ever done for me.

I will always hold dear to me, all the memories that I have had with her, and I'd like to hold on to that, for as long as I remember her, she will always live on forever within me.

Xylia Clohessy

Simone's God-daughter, aged 13

My godmother, Simone, was such a special and thoughtful person. She always remembered my birthdays and special occasions, sending me love and best wishes. I have a lovely photo of Simone and me from the day she became my godmother, which I treasure.

Even though I never got to spend enough time with Simone, I knew she was an exceptional person from my mum. She fought through all the health challenges she faced and was an inspiration to all. She achieved so much in her life, becoming a lawyer, being an advocate for organ transplants and granting wishes for sick children through charities such as 'Starlight Children's Foundation'. I only wish there could have been more time for me to get to know Simone, and for us to spend time together.

Simone loved Christmas, as do I, and we would visit her house each year to see her spectacular lights and decorations, which is such a happy memory of mine.

Not only was I lucky to have Simone as my godmother, but she was a role model to all, shining the light and way for many. I think about Simone and keep her close in my love and prayers. May she rest in peace, and may God look after her now in heaven, since she left us far too soon.

Love

Xylia

Rebecca Millen-Kok

Simone's Best Friend

The brightest stars burn the fastest so we must love them while we can.

That description, the brightest star is befitting of Simone. Shining bright and charging ahead to leave her mark on the world.

Despite her health challenges she forged ahead like all great inspirational leaders and heroes, with persistence, resilience and determination. These character traits are far more admirable, far more inspirational and led her to become a lawyer, start a Foundation, complete a Churchill Fellowship, advocate for so many and be named the Member of the Order of Australia and also nominated for the W.A. Young Australian of the year twice.

On a more personal level, it led her to act and later direct theatre productions, volunteer passionately for the Starlight Children's Foundation, travel the world and live life looking for fun, laughter and some light escapism.

She introduced me to the world of musical theatre. We saw each and every musical production that came to Perth whether it was "Chicago", "Wicked", "Rent" or "My Fair Lady", if it was coming then we were going. Her love of drama led her to drag me, with much reluctance at times, to costume parties and dress up events. This started as 15-year-olds, convincing me to enter, with her, into the school talent show as a boot-scooting duo. Never mind I'd never boot-scooted before or that it was decidedly uncool as a high schooler. Such obstacles were trivial. She worked out the choreography, by way of a boot-scooting video, roped her mum into making some fabulous costumes and we practiced until we were flawless on the night. I'm not sure there was a winner, if there was, we didn't win a prize, but we had fun and it solidified our friendship. I joked and listened, she organised weird, wonderful and at times eyebrow raising experiences and we had fun together.

We went on a number of events to raise funds for Telethon, the statewide annual fundraiser for the Perth Children's Hospital (at the time Princess Margaret Hospital) as she had performed on Telethon at the hospital and was passionate in supporting the cause. Through this we met celebrities who came to support the cause - soap stars from Home and Away (the biggest names were Melissa George and Isla Fisher). Simone being a massive "Home and Away" fan eagerly made her way to the front of the line as soon as they arrived as she was determined to meet them all. This was always the highlight of her year.

In those days we had film cameras, and I remember us as teenagers returning home bemused with a whole film roll dedicated to photos with Dr Harry Cooper who kept requesting Simone to take another photo of him. Hilarious for me, more frustrating for Simone as we almost missed meeting CBD (a Melbournian boy band with a hit song at the time) and some actors from the Australian Drama Blue Heelers. Somehow though, most of those photos ended up taken on my camera. I was never quite sure what to do with the 30 odd photos with Dr Cooper but it brings a smile to my face when I see one.

Somehow we always managed to find ourselves caught up in situations that would inevitably be made all the more memorable by Simone taking the opportunity to dramatically elevate the situation. There was the time, we went dressed as nuns (after some coercing from Simone) to a Sound of Music sing-a-long event. We went to Hungry Jacks afterwards and after being on the receiving end of more than a few confused looks and raised eyebrows, decided to make the most of it by loudly saying Grace and vocalising our gratitude for the food. Simone utilised her acting skills to give an Oscar winning performance, and we giggled and exited amongst incredulous stares.

On nights out, Simone was always looking to be part of the action. This could be dancing in cages in nightclubs, being brought up on stage to be hypnotised during a performance, nominating to do a big number at karaoke or belly dancing with the local entertainment while eating at a middle eastern restaurant.

I cannot count the times we went to a hen's night or fundraisers, and she would be one of the first brought onto the stage to become part of the risqué entertainment with male review performers. I think her initial sweet demeanour probably had them thinking she would be a placid woman who wouldn't give them much trouble but she would always surprise them, leaning into the performance and giving as good as she got, often with hilariously surprised looks from the performers. On one memorable night out, even she got more than she bargained for, as they swung her around during a tantalising strip show and she ended up putting her back out.

She made sure she worked into every conversation she could about how she got that injury much to the chagrin of her parents.

In Melbourne for her 21st birthday, we went shopping. It was July and as we weren't used to the Victorian winter chill, we were rugged up with thick black jackets, black gloves and beanies. As we slowly browsed down the main tourist streets of Melbourne, we couldn't believe it when one of the shop keepers voiced, into his microphone no less, that we shouldn't be trying to get a five finger discount. I was horrified and although Simone initially didn't know what it meant, she became so offended once I explained the implication of his statement that she started arguing with him and he tried to give it right back. It led to us marching up and down in front of that shop telling everyone about the nasty shop keeper who was accusing everyone of shoplifting. We were very successful in driving away enough of his customers, so he begrudgingly apologised and we left, not before buying from the shop next door and re-enacting the scene from 'Pretty Woman' where we showed him the sales he missed out on. We were determined to teach him a lesson on stereotyping. Simone also taught him not to underestimate someone so little.

That was often the case for Simone. I affectionately used to call her my barstool as she was so short, she was just the right size for me to lean my arm on her head. But she made sure people knew she was more than a match for them even if she looked small. Whether it was a doctor and she disagreed with their treatment plan, another board member on one of her many community groups that was proposing something absurd, or poor customer service at a restaurant, she asserted her issues, determined to make things right and be heard.

While many people know of her advocating and her leadership skills, what may not be known were some of her recreational goals she achieved. Despite her physical challenges, she travelled multiples times to the USA, Europe and interstate. Coming back with fantastic stories about meeting the New York cowboy, living it up in Vegas and visiting Disney Land and the World, determined to experience as much of life as she could.

Locally we decided we would like to experience a taste of cruise life for a long weekend. What was meant to be a 4 day holiday of laying on a cruise ship drinking cocktails (or mocktails in Simone's case) turned into a cruising nightmare, no pool (it was being renovated), a violently rocking ship where you couldn't lay down or be in constant fear of falling out of your bed or sun lounger (and spilling your drink) not to mention blocked, overflowing toilets and sinks. This led to our demands to be let off the boat. After acquiescing to our repeated requests, we were lowered down in small speed boats and taken to

Busselton (much to the delight of the cruise ship workers who had never gotten to see Busselton before). Luckily between Simone and her parents, we managed to secure a night sleeping on a yacht, enjoying the stars and free entertainment at the local yacht club. Despite the nightmare start to the long weekend, determination to not waste the trip led to an unforgettable night on a yacht and one hell of a story.

That was life with Simone. Obstacles were there but determination to live life to the fullest and not waste the time we had, led to fun, laughter and hilarious, memorable stories to share. While it didn't last nearly as long as it should, she led the brightest of lives and her life was one hell of a great story. She left the deepest of impressions and taught us all a lesson about how determination can make all kinds of things possible.

Viede Clohessy

Simone's Best Friend

My friend Simone was such an amazing, inspiring person.

Not just because of her many achievements by becoming a lawyer, setting up her Foundation… The Organ Donation and Transplant Foundation of WA, her charity work as an organ donor advocate, her numerous awards – the list goes on.

Through all her challenges, Simone had this unbelievable strength of determination and will power. It was one of her many remarkable qualities and I often thought it saw her through many hurdles so she could achieve what she did, and I truly admired her for it.

She was so bubbly and happy – full of life and go, despite the difficulties she faced. Rising not shrinking from them, she made her own, incredible pathway in life, and did so with grace.

I remember very fondly our chats (conversation came easily to Simone!) and our laughs (she was such great storyteller!) and how easily that always flowed, no matter the time between calls or seeing each other. I will always miss these special times together. When I think of it now, I can hear Simone's voice just as clearly and picture her, and it makes me happy to think she is still with me.

I also fondly remember how much she loved celebrations, birthdays and Christmas were always so special to her. I have so many memories of these happy times together, with Simone's energy being the life of the party.

Simone, I miss you, and always will. You should not have left us when you did. I wish you were here, but I know Heaven gained an angel that day and until we meet again, please know that I love you my dearest friend and that you are forever in my heart.

Emma Lenane

Simone's Best Friend

Simone was a woman of extraordinary strength, a passionate advocate for organ donation and an inspiration but most of all my best friend.

It was Feb 1999 at St Norbert College; I was the only Year 11 in a free period study class.

Not knowing anyone I decided to seek companionship from two friendly faces (Simone and Bec), what seemed like a fleeting decision at the time changed the course of my life forever.

The first thing I learnt about Simone was her cheeky personality. Her and Bec decided to convince me they were psychic; they guessed my mum's name, then my address and then my brother's name (amazing I thought) so I believed they were psychic – what I learnt further on down the track was that they'd read my St Norbert diary which contained all that information. The second thing I learnt about Simone was how very persuasive she was. Having a fear of public speaking, she somehow convinced me to host the St Norbert Junior Talent Show with her! Absolutely terrified, I stood on stage with her reading my cue cards while she naturally graced the stage putting on a marvellous performance.

We shared a love of theatre, seeing my first musical Chicago with the school's drama students. I recall Simone convincing the drama teacher to let me go as I hosted the talent show. Just watching wasn't enough for Simone, she loved her acting, I watched her in countless amateur productions, she shined so brightly on the stage. Her love for theatre took her aboard watching Broadway in London and my most enviously New York.

Nights out with Simone were always memorable, never a dull moment. From what I thought would be a quiet dinner to somehow belting out karaoke, her energy was infectious. I was her go to girl, the person she'd call when she knew no one else would go with outrageous ideas. We both loved an excuse to don a costume and attend a party or charitable event.

I saw my very first concert with Simone. She called me and said "if I can win tickets to Bardot will you come with me", I agreed thinking that it would never happen, only to hear on the radio that night that they were giving them away x 10 double passes each night for a week – I knew then it was only a matter of time before she called and said we were going. Of course, she won the tickets, then convinced me to dress up like a 90's pop star. From that moment I'm sure she figured out she could convince me to dress up as anything.

Next memorable dress up would be when she asked me to dress up as a clown and hand out lollies at a charity event, no worries that's easy, I thought, only later she followed with "would you mind if a journalist comes out to do a small article for a local paper?" I reluctantly agreed and dressed up as a clown, had my photos taken thinking this will be a small article in the middle of a small local paper, of course not, this had Simone's touch, half a page full colour article run in every local paper this press company printed. And then on the day of the event Simone asked if I would be in the photo for the West Australian, thinking again it would be a small article in the middle of the paper it turned out to be a big article on page 5.

What I treasure about Simone was her passion and desire to achieve at the next level. I remember attending the WA Young Australian of the Year Awards (any excuse to get dressed up). She won in 2006 and again in 2008. In 2008 we were on a plane to Canberra to represent W.A. in the Australia Day awards. What a whirlwind of a weekend. We packed in everything Canberra had to offer and celebrated the awards ceremony in style with our fashionable Australia flag sunglasses on.

I'll never forget the Member of the Order of Australia in 2013, I missed my bus then I got on the wrong bus and made it to the ceremony with minutes to spare before they closed the doors. I'm so glad I was there to watch you receive what I believe to me was your most truly remarkable achievement. This was only second to when Simone called me and decided she was going to finish her law degree. I thought she was crazy. I tried to tell her to put her health first, but I knew that it was falling on deaf years as it was something she wanted to achieve, and I knew nothing was going to stop her so I just cheered her on.

Whilst Simone achieved so much on a professional level the greatest part of our friendship was that we could be ourselves. We appreciated a good cheap Chinese meal, watching a movie and then talking for hours. I'd be so envious at how lucky she was at the Casino always winning something on the pokies or the money wheel. We spent so many nights playing Wii, with me trying to win against you in Carnival Games, I'd always practice so hard and somehow, she always beat me.

Christmas was our favourite time of year, I always looked forward to our annual catch up. I don't even know how the little rivalry of Christmas Lights Display started. We both started out with a small display, a few strands of lights and a couple of ornaments. Then one year Simone convinced her dad to climb on the roof and put lights up there, so off I went to the shops to add more lights to my collection. After unsuccessfully trying to convince my dad to climb on the roof, up I got on the ladder in the blistering heat of a hot summer's day and put up my lights. From then on, her display got bigger and bigger until the day she called me and told me I have to vote for her in the Western Power Christmas Lights Display, I couldn't believe it, I was so envious! After this I conceded she had the best display and from that day on looked forward to seeing her remarkable display.

Simone lived her life to the fullest, she always succeeded in whatever she set out to achieve; that is what I loved about her the most. We always had our friendly little rivalries along the way, such as who could have the biggest Pooh Bear collection and who could get the best bargain in the kids' shoe section.

Though Simone is no longer physically here her memory will live on in my heart, in the stories I tell my daughter, and in the legacy of her advocacy work where she so passionately dedicated her time to highlight the profile of organ and tissue donation.

Ray Tame

It is hard to believe it is almost a year since the loss of dear Simone, who left this world on the 11th of April last year – no doubt to pursue something far more important in the next phase of her celestial journey. I say that with confidence because Simone never did anything without certainty or purpose in her short busy time with us here on Earth.

When I first came to know her, it was as "little" Simone because she was smaller in stature than her cousins, aunties and uncles through whom I came to know her. She was small because at first her body relied on only one sub-standard kidney, but after a new donated kidney was transplanted into her body at age 11, she started to show the enormous energy and zest for life that became her trademark.

Those who knew her from birth continually told me that little Simone had a gigantic heart. Following her transplant the "little caterpillar" became a beautiful butterfly, and turned the challenge of her adversity into a life of advocacy for others in need.

She celebrated the "Gift of life" given to her by an anonymous donor by dedicating herself to help those in need of organ donation, those who have donated organs (and the families involved in this heartfelt life-saving process).

By the time I met her (mid 2000s) she was already a legend. I realised she was the young girl I'd seen years before on Telethon. Then she became a Lawyer, after doing a Bachelor of Laws at Notre Dame University, a W.A. Young Australian of the Year (twice), Member of the Order of Australia recipient and was awarded a Winston Churchill Fellowship to identify and report on "international models of organ and tissue donations" - (the youngest ever to meet the fellowship requirements).

At age 25 Simone founded The Organ Donation and Transplant Foundation of W.A. (ODAT) and was State President of Transplant Australia (W.A.) which she chaired during the inaugural of the Perth Transplant Games in 2008.

I later found out she was awarded a Prime Minister's Centenary Medal also during these years.

Every Christmas family and friends would be reminded that Simone and the McMahon household was raising funds for the Starlight Foundation and Camp Quality with their "Christmas Lights Display" that became well known on the Perth Xmas Light trail.

My own humble life brushed shoulders with many of Perth's public figures. Whenever I mentioned or introduced Simone she was already known, such was her celebrity.

Simone's Fellowship and advocacy was always staunchly devoted to those needing life-saving transplant services and their families. She believed that with appropriate sensitivity, recipients and donors should be given the opportunity to meet.

Further (where the donor was posthumous) donor families might meet a healthy surviving recipient. During her busiest years Simone had advocated a system that would make organ donation a smooth and efficient process with support for families on *both* sides of the process.

Unfortunately, reality was still far from the ideal. By 2009, Simone was in need of another transplant, but it was never provided. "The system" placed her back in the queue like so many others. Soon Simone returned to the limited world of dialysis - with the loving and constant support of her parents Jennifer and Patrick.

She continued to advocate for the needy. At one point she found herself at loggerheads with the privatised bureaucracy that was threatening to withdraw support for her because of her spirited and accurate alert to a dangerous shortfall in the system. (Her assertion was later proven to be correct, but no apology was forthcoming. Simone knew that the safety and welfare of others were at risk if she remained quiet).

The advent of COVID-19 over the next three years will be remembered by us in W.A. as "difficult". For most of us, it was liveable, but imagine a family with one member whose immune system is low and living on dialysis. Simone and her family were in permanent lockdown because they couldn't risk exposure to the outside world.

But Simone never lost her spirit, her sense of humour, or her grace. Simone turned 40 in June 2022, and I sent her a recorded message because she was still fearful of infection. At the time I was moved to tears at her beautiful spirit and refusal to bow to adversity.

On April 11th, 2023, Simone's battle with adversity ended, and she departed these troubled waters for "a better place so I know". Wherever that is, she will be kicking her heels up and rejoicing in newfound vigour, probably doing something much more important than we could ever envisage here. She joins other loved ones that have gone before, and one day we will meet again.

Simone's legacy lives on in the work she undertook, and the Foundation she established to the benefit of transplant recipients, their donors and the families involved. She would exhort all of us to register for organ donation and actively support those less fortunate than ourselves through volunteering or contribution.

God bless you, Simone. RIP.

Nannette Pethick

Simone's Year 3 Primary School Teacher

I had the privilege of meeting and teaching Simone when she attended Notre Dame Catholic Primary School in Cloverdale, in the 90s. She was one of many year 3 students, but over the years she has become so much more. Teachers don't have favourites, but I can tell you the little girl that I taught in Year 3 melted my heart with her infectious smile and her zest for life, despite the challenges and hurdles she faced from such a young age. Simone was a friendly, vivacious and kind little girl. She was very much loved and supported by our small school community, particularly when she received her kidney transplant.

Simone had a profound impact on those around her and drew a lot of positive attention when she wrote a speech about recycling. Not recycling rubbish, but recycling organs, and what a lasting impression she had on the lives of so many, even from such a young age.

Steve Doohan, another teacher at the school, was also a favourite of Simone's in primary school, and I could feel a bit of friendly rivalry developing. In true diplomatic style, we both were allowed to carry the title. I was her favourite female teacher and Steve, her favourite male teacher.

The year after I taught Simone, I was married and she, along with other students, made my wedding day even more special by their presence. Simone's mum Jennifer actually made our wedding cake, and I remember Simone telling me it would be the best I ever tasted!

Fast forward to 2002 and Simone nominated our terminally ill daughter Melissa for a wish through the Starlight Children's Foundation, an organisation close to her heart. She visited our family in hospital and served as a beacon of hope and courage. I remember thinking how inspirational she was, and how proud I was of her, and the unwavering dedication she displayed to things she was passionate about.

I wasn't surprised when she was given the honour of being young Western Australian of the year twice, and I must confess that I have said on numerous occasions, "I taught Simone McMahon" and consider that it was both an honour and a privilege to stay connected to her throughout her life.

I attended a celebratory dinner when Simone was awarded a Member of the Order of Australia and again it was another amazing achievement, that was a testimony to her hard work and dedication to help others.

I am a natural redhead and a primary school teacher, I love to wear bright colours but there are two colours you will never see in my wardrobe, and they are red and pink, and yet I attended Simone's funeral in the brightest pink top I could find.

If I had the opportunity to speak to Simone one more time, I would tell her that she is officially my favourite student, but I suspect, or at least I hope she already knew that. I would thank her for making such a positive impact in my life, and for leaving her footprints on my heart.

I truly believe that Simone's spirit and legacy will live on in the hearts and minds of all those that knew and loved her, and that she will continue to guide us all. Finally, I would like to share a short verse I wrote. It is my parting message to you Simone.

Footprints in the sand

Last mere seconds in a day,

Inevitably the waves come crashing in

And they get washed away.

The footprints you left Simone

Are etched deep in my heart

And they will remain there forever

Even though we are apart.

Times shared with you are engraved in my memory.

And they will never wash away,

You are imprinted on my soul Simone.

And I'll carry you in my heart every day.

NP

Reflection of an Angel by Steve Doohan

Teacher Notre Dame Primary School

I met Simone as a student at Notre Dame Catholic Primary School, in my then role as schoolteacher.

Little did I realise, that this beautiful little girl with her zest for happiness and an incredible sense of humour, would in time eventually exchange roles with me as she taught me the lessons of dealing with adversity and accepting life's challenges head on – that you get up and "do" and even when wounded, you persevere and fight the good fight – and She did. I bow to my teacher... Simone.

Reflections on Simone by Jenneth Stibi

St. Norbert College

My first memories of Simone are from her time as a student at St. Norbert College where I was serving as a Deputy Principal. Simone was a vibrant member of the College Community, and I was always in awe of her courage and resilience. She just got on with her studies and threw herself into the life of the school regardless of the challenges she faced.

We stayed in touch after she left school, and I followed her studies and career into law. She always generously gave her time with the help of her beautiful parents, to speak to students about her life and work in the promotion of organ donation. Students loved her engaging style, sense of fun, and authenticity.

I was thrilled when she received a Churchill Fellowship and was awarded the honour of W.A. Young Australian of the Year. It was exciting and a great privilege to be included in the celebrations the night her Member of the Order of Australia was announced.

Simone's Christmas cards and messages of support throughout the years, was a testament to her caring nature. I loved voting for the family Christmas lights each year!

Simone will be remembered by me, as a young woman with a huge zeal for life which was so infectious. Her care, compassion, and commitment to the work of organ donation promotion was phenomenal. Above all, her courage and ability to stay positive and connected through so many years of adversity is truly inspirational.

Simone and the love of her parents will never be forgotten.

John Hammond

Director, Hammond Legal

I had the privilege of being Simone's lawyer through a very difficult time in Simone's life.

During that time, I had many conversations with Simone about life, the law, fighting for what she believed was right, the health system (its failings and its successes), and organ donation.

Simone struck me as kind, sincere, and above all else, someone who wanted to ensure that people were treated fairly and humanely.

Whilst Simone won numerous awards for her contribution to Western Australia's less fortunate, Simone was passionate about organ donation.

I am also a keen advocate for organ donation and shared Simone's desire to make organ donation something society undertook on a routine basis.

Simone was stoic.

Many people, other than her family and closest confidantes, did not know that Simone spent countless hours receiving dialysis. Up to 4 hours a day were spent hooked to a dialysis machine, either at a hospital or, in the later years, at home.

Notwithstanding this massive imposition on her daily life, Simone was not deterred in her fight for dialysis patients to have better access to dialysis both at home and at the hospital.

I might have forgotten to mention that Simone did obtain a law degree along the way, win a Winston Churchill scholarship, and become the CEO of the Organ Donation and Transplant Foundation.

As a former Chair of the Heart & Lung Transplant Foundation, I understood the commitment that Simone was making.

However, you can never overlook what Simone had to overcome to achieve these goals – the constant uncertainty in relation to her health, the thousands of hours of dialysis each year, the medical appointments, and the pain.

All in all, Simone was a brave woman.

Pip Brennan

Consumer Advocate, Former Executive Director of the Health Consumers' Council.

It started with what seemed like a very valid and straightforward advocacy request. As a woman having to manage home and community dialysis, she wanted to have choice about the tubing that was used for this life-saving procedure. She had valid, documented reasons for her preferences. I followed the thread of the issue as raised to the Health Consumers' Council, where I was Executive Director at the time. It led to a giant ball of string of impactful, advocacy of the scale and breadth that impressed and frankly staggered me.

I knew Simone was tackling grave health issues on a daily basis, yet I discovered just how tireless she was in her efforts to improve our health system. She was the embodiment of the consumer whose passion for research and exhaustive knowledge of a topic reflected that it had life-and-death implications for her.

There were so many skills and talents Simone brought to the issue. She was a qualified lawyer among other things and ran the Organ Donation and Transplant Foundation of W.A. She was the youngest person to complete a Churchill Fellowship and had contributed significantly as a younger person to give voice to the experience of youth impacted by kidney disease. In so many ways - as a volunteer, as an ambassador, as a professional - she was dedicated to championing the safety and quality improvements for patients requiring organ donation and support for kidney disease.

After reviewing the issue Simone brought to the Health Consumers' Council, it raised a number of issues I hadn't previously thought of and alerted me to systemic issues that I would need to monitor. From my perspective, the service in question did not behave in a way that is consistent with putting the patient first. Together, we reminded them of the primacy of patient safety and experience and put them "on notice."

I was so saddened to hear of Simone's death - she was incredibly vital and determined it seemed hard to believe. There are some people you meet through your work that you never forget.

Simone is one of those people. She has left an enormous, positive legacy in the organ donation and transplant sector and will be forever missed.

Cassie Rowe

MLA – State Member for Belmont

I had the privilege to know Simone for a number of years. I was always struck by her incredibly happy disposition, and perennial drive to make sure others wouldn't have to go through what she went through in her health journey. She had such obvious intelligence, and a deep abiding moral compass that drove her to seek justice.

Simone's unwavering advocacy for organ transplantation is a testament to her selfless character and her genuine compassion. Simone's volunteer work for Kidney Health Australia, as well as her role as CEO of the Organ Donation and Transplant Foundation truly shows her commitment to representing the lives of those in need of organs.

Simone's dedication to donor advocacy did not go unnoticed, receiving high accolades such as the award of the Member of Australia. I had the privilege of meeting Simone where I was deeply inspired by her activism and developed a special understanding of her experience with the organ donor process.

On behalf of Simone and her family, I have personally reached out to the Western Australian Minister for Health urging for reforms that will make the organ transplant process more accessible and efficient. I was only made aware of these issues due to Simone's own experience and her advocacy for all donors.

Simone built a legacy on compassion, strength and selflessness. That will always be remembered.

Ben Wyatt

Former Treasurer, Western Australia

Simone was, without a doubt, one of the most caring, determined and positive people I had the very good fortune in getting to know during my time in Parliament.

I first met Simone not long after she had been recognised as the W.A. Young Australian of the Year and, over the years, I found Simone to be a fierce advocate for those seeking organ transplants. Her gentle demeanour was never to be confused with her own desire to advocate for those who relied upon her voice, and this was recognised time and again with public awards.

Simone had such an extraordinary impact on all those who had the very good fortune to come within her orbit.

Chris Thomas

CEO, Transplant Australia

Very rarely in our lives do we meet someone who exhibits the qualities of humanity to which we all wish to aspire. Graciousness, positivity, courage, empathy, and above all, determination beyond all logic.

Simone McMahon was one such person. A young lady gone before her time but a person who left an indelible mark on the lives of all those she touched.

I first met Simone in 2007, and we shared many robust conversations, on how to improve the lives of transplant recipients. We both had our perspectives, and our approaches sometimes differed, however, we both deeply respected each other's opinions.

Seventeen years on, as CEO of Transplant Australia, I owe a debt of gratitude to Simone for helping me better understand the ongoing journey, including setbacks from time to time, of organ recipients.

She experienced all the highs of someone who made the most of her transplant – rising to the National Board of Transplant Australia, achieving a Churchill Fellowship and establishing her own W.A. state-based charity promoting donation.

And she, sadly, experienced the lows of losing a transplant, however she faced this time with great dignity. And right behind her struggles, fighting every step of the way, were her wonderful parents Jennifer and Patrick.

I was honoured to be asked to speak at Simone's funeral. I prayed that day that Patrick and Jennifer would find peace, knowing they could not love their daughter more.

Perhaps with this book it is time to celebrate Simone's life. Not be sad that she is gone but be thankful she graced this earth even for just a short time.

Sue Nash

Former DonateLife Community Council Member and Lawyer

I first met Simone at a meeting of the W.A. DonateLife Community Council in December 2013. I had joined the Council after my sister had died from leukaemia waiting for a stem cell transplant. Miraculously, my brother and I were both a perfect tissue match for her and I could not understand why she had died waiting for a transplant. I saw an ad in the paper for volunteers for the DonateLife Council and wanted to help.

When I first met Simone, I was struck by this pint-sized, radiant, bubbly dynamo who commanded the room. Simone clearly had immense personal experience and knowledge about organ and tissue transplantation and donation, whereas I had none. She helped me to understand the issues faced by transplant recipients in W.A.

She was a terrific Council member - friendly, respectful and helpful -and contributed enthusiastically to every meeting she attended, even when she was not feeling well. She always had a flower in her hair and was immaculately dressed (with the cutest shoes!). Her beautiful smile and friendly nature raised my spirits whenever I saw her.

Simone was part of our DonateLife working group trying to reinstate organ donation status on drivers' licences as the easiest way to get people to sign up to register as donors. I think her AM status gave us credibility. We met with State government officials, who were helpful and receptive to the idea, but after some time working on the project, we discovered that our efforts had been futile as (at that time) there was no federal Minister for Transplant support.

Over the next few years, Simone asked me to assist her with a few personal legal battles. She had enough hardship in her life without other people making things harder, but she was always up for a fight. Her energy and tenacity in the face of adversity amazed me. She was not afraid of anyone when fighting the good fight, even if that might have made her unpopular.

Simone told me how much she enjoyed working as a lawyer. She was made for the job. Although she had immense problems completing her restricted practice year because of the need to be on dialysis, she persevered and found a job she loved.

Simone was very proud of her family's Christmas lights. Their efforts each year made people happy and raised money for charity. What wonderful parents to go through so much, raise such an exceptional daughter and still think about others.

Life is a journey of learning. What I learned with gratitude from Simone was that we can inspire others by being brave and living a meaningful life. Despite her tiny stature and everything she had to endure; Simone lifted others up. She was truly heroic.

Bruce Powell

Our paths crossed during my time as Medical Director of Organ and Tissue Donation in Western Australia. Simone was brave. More than that, she was fierce, determined, tough, bloody-minded. She was exactly what she had to be, to survive all the trials of her life. A tiny form with a huge personality. It was an honour to have known Simone. When I battle with my own challenges, I think of her and remind myself that it is possible to fight on, scrap it out.

That was Simone. Brave, brave Simone.

Melissa Dumitru

My beautiful friend Simone is now resting with our Lord's angels.

It has been my sincerest pleasure to have worked with her and her incredible parents.

A true reflection of service to our community and people living with chronic illness and needing transplants.

Simone was a warrior, whose quiet strength benefited so many.

Her lived experience has left a legacy that few people living with such great adversity are usually able to do.

We are so blessed to have had her in our lives.

Thank you for carrying out the good fight, my friend.

Now rest and know that we will see you again in Heaven.

To your gorgeous parents, please be assured that those who know and love you all, know who you are and what the whole truth is. Never doubt that you followed the right path for Simone.

Thank you, Simone, for your incredible service to so many.

We are so grateful to have had you in our lives and to have enjoyed so many great times.

Footnote:

Simone's dear friend Melissa sadly passed away shortly after Simone in November 2023. The two tireless community workers are now together in Heaven.

Tom Mone

One Legacy, Southern Carolina, U.S.A.

I was CEO of One Legacy, the organ recovery organisation serving Southern California from 2000–2022. I am now the Chief External Officer at One Legacy. I was a speaker at the National Organ Donation Conference in Adelaide in 2006, The World Transplant Conference in Sydney in 2008, and was an advisor to the Australian Donate Life Program in Melbourne and Canberra in 2013.

Has it been 20 years since I first met Simone McMahon and a decade since I saw her? Probably right... and we probably met face to face only two or three times over those years... but Simone was regularly in my thoughts and always among my most admired transplant advocates.

When we met, I was amazed, intrigued, and inspired by her very apparent joy for life, dedication to the cause of increasing organ donation and transplants, and the ability to bring people from the donation, transplant, dialysis, and political worlds together.

As time passed, I saw Simone's fingerprints on efforts to improve donation and access to transplants to all Australians and people in need worldwide....and I knew that the work was in good hands.

On my last visit to Australia, I had the pleasure of briefly meeting Simone's parents and her source of her attitude, people skills and talents became clear... the apple didn't fall far from the tree. Of course, we are not just clones or products of our parents....and the rarest among us take the best, and leave the rest, and create a life guided by a "why", a purpose, and become their own person who makes a difference in the world... Simone was that person, and we are all better for her time here with us.

Lucy Scott

Volunteer, Organ Donation and Transplant Foundation of W.A.

Simone McMahon was an incredible force in the realm of organ donation. As the founder and CEO of the Organ Donation and Transplant Foundation of Western Australia, Simone was dedicated and passionate in her mission to deliver community education, promotion, support, and advocacy on all aspects of organ and tissue donation. Simone will be remembered for her unwavering dedication to enhancing the lives of West Australians in need of organ and tissue donations and their families.

I consider myself fortunate to have joined Simone at the Organ Donation and Transplant Foundation of W.A. during a pivotal stage of my life. I was fresh out of university, with a degree in health promotion, and eager to make a difference and we worked together to organise a "New Life" art and photography exhibition during Donate Life week at a busy local shopping centre. The exhibition showcased stories of hope and transformation, bringing the power of organ donation to the forefront of the community's attention. Simone's mentorship and wisdom helped shape the trajectory of my career in public health, she pushed me to be bolder, more assertive, and unapologetically confident in my abilities as I sought opportunities in the field.

Simone's dedication to the cause of organ donation was both profound and inspiring. Her annual "Star Night" event stands out vividly – an evening dedicated to celebrating the "Gift of Life". Simone orchestrated the gathering each year in partnership with the Perth Observatory's Adopt a Star program, bringing together donor families for a night of remembrance under the canopy of the night sky. Each star dedicated on those nights highlighted the spirit of giving, honouring all W.A. organ and tissue donors who had given the ultimate "gift of life". The event was conducted with utmost respect, an atmosphere highly appreciated by all those donor families who attended.

Simone's fundraising prowess was legendary, encompassing a diverse array of events from quiz nights, movie nights, sausage sizzle fundraisers, and sales of the entertainment books, to uplifting music art and theatre performances. Through her tireless efforts, she transformed mere concepts into tangible realities. The continual success of these endeavours was a testament to her resourcefulness and ingenuity in rallying support.

Simone's commitment to nurturing future leaders was always evident in her support of untold volunteers, as well as university students from the John Curtin Leadership Academy, inspiring the next generation to carry forward her legacy of compassion and advocacy.

Simone championed the importance of open dialogue with loved ones about organ donation, recognising that true change begins with conversation and understanding, even as she herself awaited a transplant, Simone remained steadfast in her mission, her resilience shining through adversity.

Simone will be remembered as a catalyst for change and an inspiration to those who had the privilege of knowing her. Her work has left a positive impact on countless lives.

Andrew Baker

Simone started at Notre Dame University Law School the same day as me. I think we all noticed her unique stature and energy immediately. This was in the days before laptop ubiquity, so we all lugged around extremely hefty (and expensive) legal textbooks to every class. This was at the very least an irritating task, but often it was downright taxing. Simone, even with her petite frame, always seemed to be smiling and beaming a positive energy whilst juggling the collection of law tomes in her bag upstairs, across courtyards, and over busy Fremantle streets. She was utterly irrepressible. It wasn't just the physical challenge of the books, she also remained upbeat with each, and every new academic challenge thrown at us as we all made our way towards our LLB. Simone was always the most delightful presence in our classes – she was great to have around.

As well as sharing a university degree, Simone and I also had a mad passion for all things musical theatre. She had gone to a high school with a strong drama program like I had – she was mentored by the amazing Kerri Hilton of course! -so we had a lot in common. I think by the time we met; she may have been over east more than I had. She got to see more shows than I had. I'd only dream of seeing in person. I think she may have also been to Broadway by then, but I know she went again further down the track. I was extremely jealous. She was one of the few people in my life at the time who understood and spoke my language of musical theatre. We connected over that. We talked about every new show that was opening on Broadway or coming to Perth. She came to see me in a couple of productions I was in, and then we worked together on "Grease" at the Regal. She was an Assistant Stage Manager, and I have such fond memories of seeing Simone beaming from the wings. She was a committed and hard-working member of the team. I know she had other great experiences being a part of shows across Perth, too.

Some years later Simone rang me to talk about establishing what was to become the Organ Donation and Transplant Foundation of W.A. I had been a lawyer for a short time but didn't have many skills to help to be honest. But we worked through some of the incorporation options together and I think she ended up getting expert assistance. I was honoured she had reached out, though.

She seemed to be fighting her transplant system battle, and I largely thought nothing would come of the ambition to establish this new charity. Well, I really should have known by then never to doubt Simone McMahon. What she established was real and needed. When I visited her Maylands offices. I was nearly brought to tears by the humble but also substantial magnitude of it all. She had a team, infrastructure and a program up and running. Simone was proud but busy, all too aware of the challenges she faced. Her work in that space is an extraordinary legacy and testament to that tenacity I first witnessed in the year 2000 when Simone refused to let those heavy books win.

I'm very proud to have known Simone and I often think of her example of a life well-lived. I will never forget her.

Marija Jelavic

I can remember my first meeting with Simone. I went back to my office breathless and thought I have met a "human dynamo".

To be in her company was to be in awe – she was small in stature but a huge personality who touched everyone she knew in deep, surprisingly and profound ways.

She did not let her illness define her. She got on with life and pursued her academic and career goals. Working with her was inspirational. She led by example and was an irresistible force as she set the direction. We planned, we discussed, we debated, and laughed, and she always had time for a coffee (even though she didn't drink it).

She was intelligent, funny, kind, generous, caring and fearless. She was full of passion, loyal, yet fierce. She had a rare ability to connect with people at any level.

Simone's incredible energy and spirit will live on through her work that made such a difference in the lives of many people, her beloved family and those of us who were fortunate enough to be considered her friends.

Dave Reid

I first met Simone back in 2013. I was still relatively new to my business, and she had called to ask for a quote on some signs for her new office in Burswood. I found her immediately likable, and we hit it off straight away.

She would call from time to time to arrange for some extra stickers or a banner for her foundation, the Organ Donation and Transplant Foundation of W.A. and I was always happy to hear from her and help where I could. Simone always seemed above her struggles, she was obviously a fighter, and her slight stature belied her inner strength.

It was a gift to know her and while we didn't see each other too often it was always nice to hear from her. She was a credit to her parents and hearing her friends and colleagues speak so highly of her at her funeral was no surprise.

Simone will always remain in my thoughts with fondness.

John Dore

Neighbour

I moved to Pontiac Avenue in 1986 with my wife Anne and two young children Lisa and John. Simone was four at that time.

We gradually made friends with the McMahons and our relationship grew stronger through the years.

We had the pleasure of watching Simone develop into a very astute, smart, brave and beautiful young lady.

With all the health problems Simone had to cope with she kept her cheeky personality and great sense of humour.

My wife Anne passed away in 2012. Her last social outing was Simone's New York themed birthday party. A very happy occasion and enjoyed by all.

In 2017, I found love again with my partner Lesley. When introduced to Simone, Jen and Patrick they opened their arms to her and warmly welcomed her to the family.

Everyone who has met Simone and has gotten to know her have come away the better person from the experience,

Rest in peace Simone.

Always across the Road.

Neroli Sweetman

Director, Community Theatre

It is my privilege to share my memories of Simone from when I first met her at a community theatre audition I was holding for the musical "South Pacific", which was to be performed in the beautiful Old Mill Theatre in South Perth in 2006. As the Director of a production, we start by auditioning for all those budding Actors and Actresses who present themselves in the hopes they will be chosen to become part of the cast. Simone was one of these young artists, and after auditioning was chosen to become an "Island Girl" in the ensemble cast. She quickly showed an ability to take direction and from memory, this was the first Community Theatre production that she had been a part of. Her personality and friendliness meant that she slotted quickly into the production and the theatre family. She also introduced another member of her own family, "Brittany" to audition for the part of one of Emily de Becque's two children and Brittany too became part of the "South Pacific" team.

It was a beautiful production, although the role Simone played was not a major role, she quickly proved to be an integral cast member.

In 2010, the Old Mill Theatre production was "Fiddler on the Roof". This show required quite a large cast, and I was very pleased when Simone and Patrick, her father, auditioned once again. Patrick became one of the "Papas" and Simone showed her talent as one of the "Mamas" and also the role of the "Beggar". Character parts definitely suited her, and it was lovely to see her make each one her own.

The next time I had the pleasure of welcoming Simone into a production was in 2012 when I directed "Scrooge" for the Melville Theatre Company, she became one of the adult chorus members and played the part of "Polly" and to prove that theatre does bring families together, we were lucky to also have Simone's father Patrick audition for us once again, we welcomed them both to the team.

Moving forward another year and back at the Old Mill Theatre for this season a pantomime "Snow White", once again Simone and Patrick auditioned and were cast. In this fun show Simone played two roles again, "Beatrix Potter" and "Barry Trotter" one of the comedy roles of the production. To play pantomime is very different to musical productions and Simone's portrayal of "Barry Trotter" gained much laughter, and applause from the audience who attended.

From the beginning of Simone's involvement in the theatre, we were aware of the amazing young woman she was, and the health issues she suffered, and we were in awe of her accomplishments throughout her life. She made many friends during her time in Community Theatre, and I valued her contribution to the productions I directed.

Kerri Hilton

Drama Teacher, St. Norbert College

Simone McMahon was my student to start with and later, my friend.

I met Simone as a year 8 student. A very small framed young lady with a heart bigger than she was.

Simone did well at school academically, but she was always looking for more. She thrived in drama classes, and it was there that she found her outlet for her passions of speaking and performing. She truly loved theatre in all forms.

She would always audition for everything, she would go out of her way to be at every rehearsal, she would have her lines learned, and was always so diligent. I got to know Simone through upper school drama and drama clubs and ex-student productions. She was always looking out for others and always wanted to do the best for her parents. Her parents clearly adored her, and she adored them, and would do anything for them.

She was such a hard worker in everything she did. She had an infectious laugh, she had a strong moral compass, and she had a vision for what she could do to help the world, one person at a time.

It was astonishing to see Simone work and to see how she threw herself into everything. She certainly taught me many things and for that I will always be grateful.

Simone fought a good courageous fight even when she felt she couldn't go on, she did.

I am blessed and honoured to have known Simone and to have counted her as a dear friend,

George Formentin

Volunteer, Organ Donation and Transplant Foundation of W.A.

I came across Simone at a time when I was working with her mum, Jennifer. After I got to know Jennifer, it was only a short matter of time before she started telling me about this amazing daughter she had. Simone had been awarded the Churchill Fellowship where she got to travel the world and look at how other countries manage their organ donation affairs. Simone was studying Law and seemed to have a string of amazing accomplishments that went on and on. And how Jennifer loved to tell me about them all and send me news articles and pictures!

When I met Simone, I could not believe how such a big personality could fit in such a small person. She had charisma in truckloads and man... could she talk!!!

Jennifer told me Simone hated her name being mispronounced to "Simon". When a doctor once called out "Simon", she just ignored him until he got the pronunciation right!! Well, when I heard that I started calling her "Simon", she retaliated immediately, calling me "Georgina" instead of George!

My father was a philanthropist, and I was interested in learning more about The Organ Donation and Transplant Foundation charity that Simone had established. So before long, I was volunteering at her fund-raising event. The regulars were sausage sizzles at Bunnings, "The Star Night" that Simone had started to recognise the families of organ donors and thank them for acknowledging the wishes of their family members and saving lives through the "Gift of Life". The event was held with the help of the Perth Observatory, near Dumas House, and also an event at Government House and a Quiz Night.

I would help where I could, but this was usually setting up or cooking at the sausage sizzle stand. I joked with Simone that I expected to be received at the Governor's house on the red carpet. To my surprise she arranged it for me. She was never far away, and she was always a lot of fun. I had a lot of fun teasing Simone, her family, and her staff at Organ Donation and Transplant Foundation of W.A.

Simone just rose to the occasion when it came to public speaking, she was a natural and you could see that she just loved it. Speaking was one of her favourite things. I had dinner at her place one night, and she spoke to me for two hours straight before drawing breath. It was such a challenge for me to just stay focused. I really miss those days they were so much fun.

I feel so much for the struggle that was Simone's life. It seems that everything was against her, yet she persisted "with a smile" despite what seemed to be an endless barrage of setbacks.

The Organ Donation and Transplant Foundation of W.A. was established by Simone to promote organ donation, because in this country there is only a small number of organ and tissues available, while there is a long list of people needing organ and tissue transplants.

I do believe removing the organ donation tick box from the drivers' licence application made matters worse. Even worse when an organ donation is available, doctors must ask the permission of relatives if the deceased person's wishes can be carried out. I really feel that it's all too easy for the relatives to say no.

If the way this was administered was altered a little, it could make a substantial difference. For example, instead of requiring a yes or no answer, I believe the relatives should be asked if they desire to overturn their loved ones wishes then they would need to complete some forms outlining the reasons why.

However, I feel the only action that would resolve this decision once and for all is to implement an owner onus system. A system that registers all citizens as donors by default, and anyone who does not want to be on the list can ask to have their name removed. However, a government policy change is needed for this, and attaining a political bill is an onerous task.

Simone's work in this area and others like her will aggregate to eventually bring about positive change. I trust in God that one day this will become a reality.

God bless you, Simone.

Photos of Simone's Life

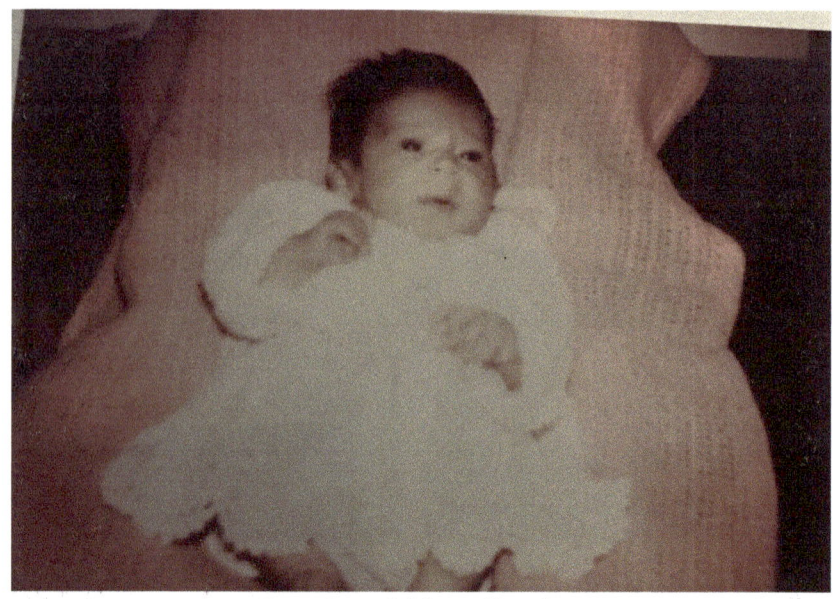

One day old bundle of joy

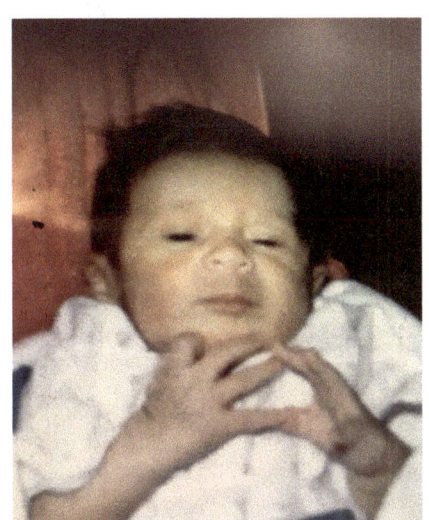

Simone looks like she already had great plans

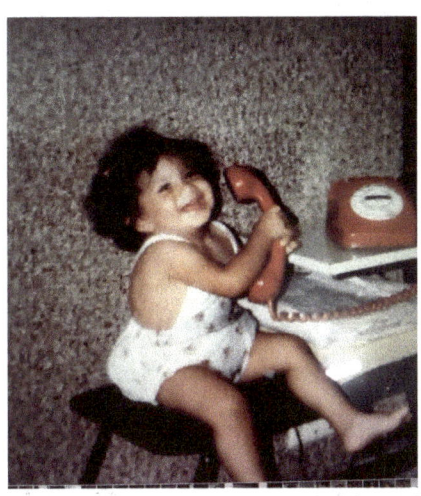

Baby Simone is one year old and already talking fluently

People called her a walkie-talkie doll

Little Simone and her favourite toy Fat Cat

Simone with her beautiful almond shaped eyes

The brilliant young lawyer

W.A. Young Australian of The Year 2006

W.A. Young Australian of the Year 2008 with Prime Minister Kevin Rudd at the Australia Day Awards.

Lions Courage Award from Governor Michael Jeffery

Simone receiving the Member of the Order of Australia from Governor Malcolm McCusker

Simone's transplant games medals – 1 gold, 3 silvers and 2 bronze

Carrying in the Commonwealth Games Flag as W.A.'s Young Australian of the Year (Simone on the right)

Simone with The Queens Baton Relay XXI Commonwealth Games

The Queens Baton Relay XXI Commonwealth Games

The Winston Churchill Trust

Simone McMahon, was twelve years old when she needed a kidney transplant. In her mid-twenties she started the Organ Donation and Transplant Foundation of Western Australia, after becoming the 3,000th Churchill Fellow

At Madame Tussaud's Wax Museum with her favourite, Sir Winston Churchill

At Madame Tussaud's Wax Museum with Benny Hill

Playing Barry Trotter

Simone at her piano

Simone's famous High Teas for her mum on Mother's Day, complete with menu

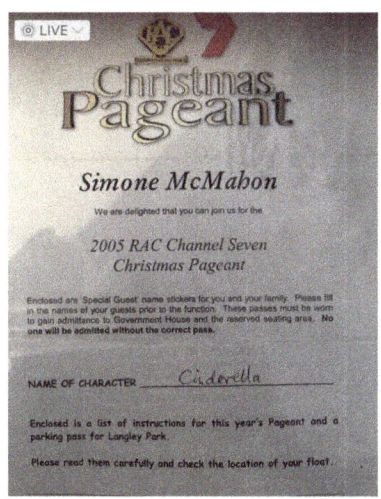

The Christmas Pageant – Simone was Cinderella much to her delight

Simone's Christmas table decorations

Simone's Easter table decorations

In Venice

*Simone's favourite place –
Times Square*

Simone's well-known Christmas lights

Simone's famous Nativity Set

The last Christmas Lights Simone put up in 2022

Thank you note from a long time Christmas Lights enthusiast

The entertaining little magician

Simone eating her favourite potato tornado

Simone's favorite past time enjoying the beach

Simone loved lazing at the pool in her free time

Simone on her 40th birthday

Another happy photo of Simone on her birthday

Simone on her 40th Birthday with her Happy Birthday sign given by her aunt and uncle

Simone's garden filled with little Winnie the Pooh ornaments given by her friends for her 40th birthday

Simone with John Farnham

Simone at the John Farnham concert

Simone and Sir Cliff Richard

Simone and Celine Dion

Simone and her friend Viede

Emma and Simone at the Australia Day Awards in Canberra

Simone and her friends Emma and Rebecca

Simone and Rebecca

Simone with Viede at her wedding

Simone with Emma and Rebecca

Simone and Nanny

Simone and her dad in lockdown

Simone and her god-daughter and cousin Lesley-Ann

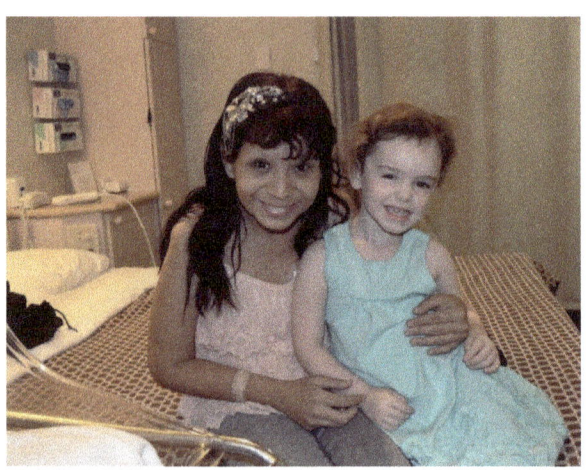

Simone and her god-daughter Xylia

Simone at the Wildcats Game with Wilbur

Wild Cats buddies Simone and her Dad

Simone and her Dad with matching Christmas clothing

Simone and her loving mum

Simone at 2 years old with her loving parents

Simone and her adoring parents

They say love begins in a moment, grows over time and lasts for an eternity

Jen and Patrick say they do believe that love definitely lasts for an eternity, as since Simone left they have experienced different incidents where Simone makes her presence felt, to comfort her very heart-broken parents.

To name just a few incidents...

Simone frequently changes the radio station in the car. Another occasion was when Jen and Patrick had just gone to bed after what was one of their "grief days" when they were really missing Simone. The dining room radio came on and her favourite singer John Farnham was singing.

Just after Simone left in April, her parents were struggling to cope on the 9th of June, Simone's birthday. So, family members organised a get-together for breakfast in Simone's memory. While driving back home from breakfast, Patrick tearfully said, "Please baby, I wish you can show us you are here. We are really missing you today on your birthday".

Patrick decided to stop and fill up fuel, but suddenly the fuel pump stopped working while he was filling the car. Patrick asked Jen to call the attendant, but when Jen looked at the pump, she noticed the pump had stopped at 1982... Simone's year of birth. Jen says she told Patrick, "Simone has answered your question. She is here with us. Look at the pump". Patrick saw the 19.82 and knew then that was a message from Simone. Patrick paid the $19.82, but they waited to see the next person fill up fuel just to confirm if the pump would work again, and it did work.

They realised then that Simone was definitely letting them know she was with them for her birthday. Jen quickly took a photo of the pump, as she could not believe it herself! They say they had to go back the next day to fill the car up again.

Jen and Patrick say they gain immense comfort knowing that their precious daughter is still with them and as said "love is truly an eternal flame, once lit it will continue to burn forever".

The couple say they are familiar that messages do come from beyond, and first learnt about these messages from loved ones from beyond in 2011 when Jen lost her two younger brothers in their 40s, the same age as Simone. They say "family is the anchor that holds us through life's storms" and Jen and Patrick recall an incident that taught them that the bonds of family ties are never broken if they are strong enough. Simone's two young uncles, who left this world in their 40s, both loved Simone as much as she loved them.

So what transpired in 2011 when Simone was in ICU was unbelievable... but understandable!!

Simone was in ICU on a ventilator and could not be woken on the first attempt. The terrified parents were informed they would try the next day to wake Simone up. When Jen and Patrick arrived at ICU the next day, they were met by a young nurse who said "Simone had two young male visitors at 9.00 pm late that night". The parents were confused and asked the young nurse to describe the young male visitors. The nurse said gushingly, "tall, dark and handsome and I wouldn't mind their phone numbers!".

Jen recalls looking at the young nurse as she described the visitors. The nurse did not understand why the parents were looking so troubled, but the parents couldn't tell the young nurse that she was describing Jen's two young brothers who had just passed away. Jen and Patrick said they began to panic that the uncles had come for Simone! They say they were so relieved when Simone woke up and said, "Mum, Uncle Leslie was in one ear singing 'Tiny Bubbles' and Uncle Richard was in my other ear yelling, 'wake up!'"

Simone went on to say how her Uncle Leslie always sang 'Tiny Bubbles' whenever she had anaesthetic. Simone said Uncle Richard was yelling for her to wake up because she was frightening her parents. Some things in life remain unexplainable...and as they say...

Love really does transcend beyond eternity.

Jen and Patrick are confident that their beautiful daughter Simone has not left them and will always be there to protect them and sustain them through their darkest days.